PRAISES FO

"There is a difference between a Travel Agent and a Tour Guide. A Travel Agent can send you on a journey she may have never taken herself. She knows about it via books, pictures, videos, word of mouth, etc. However, a Tour Guide has "been there – done that." She knows the terrain from personal experience. FIGHTING FOR YOUR DESTINY is not written by a Travel Agent. Pastor Gary Hawkins, Sr. is truly a Tour Guide – he's been there – done that. This book could be hazardous to your future. You may become a warrior fighting for your destiny."

Dr. Samuel R. Chand,
President, Beulah Heights Bible College,
Atlanta, Georgia

"Many people dream, but never achieve their dreams because they lose focus. Dreams must never be attached to people, places or things, but to God. In this great book, "Fighting For Your Destiny" Pastor Hawkins tells the real story, for real dreamers, about God's role in our experiencing our destiny."

Christopher Chappell,
Pastor, Grace Community Baptist Church,
Marietta, Georgia

"In this book Pastor Gary Hawkins, Sr. has written a masterpiece for those pastors who think that they have come to the end of their road in the pursuit of achieving their God given vision for ministry. He pushes you to another level in God by his example and unwavering faith. Bishop E. Bernard Jordan says, "Destiny is not left up to chance, it is a matter of choice". Pastor Gary Hawkins, Sr. has made a deliberate choice to fight for his destiny. He's not waiting for a chance, but opportunities to seize the moment to go after those things which God has placed in his heart. If you are going to fight for your destiny, this book gives you encouragement, enlightenment, and inspiration to never settle for less than what God told you in spite of what your situation looks like. Your destiny is worth fighting for!"

Dr. Larry D. Manning,
Bishop, New Life Ministries,
Valdosta, Georgia

"*Fighting For Your Destiny* is an anointed work of God by an anointed man of God. Gary Hawkins, Sr. both instructs and challenges the reader in the awesome destiny God has purposed for His people. This book is built on a strong biblical foundation and unbelievably practical in its application. The faithful reader will find a virtual guidebook to overcoming the challenges of life and directions to walking in victory. The chapter on *A Soldier's Mindset* alone is worth the price of the book. The believer is taken from boot camp to battleground in a profound yet practical strategy under girded by the Word of God. Whether you are a new believer or a long time leader in the church, *Fighting for Your Destiny* has a message to strengthen and enlighten you."

Raymond A. Jetson,
Pastor, Star Hill Baptist Church,
Baton Rouge, Louisiana

"God has heard the cry from the body of Christ; a clamoring for direction and guidance as we seek to walk in Kingdom excellence and integrity. As we move away from the Egyptian shadows of fear and timidity, I bless God for one of the twenty-first century "Joshua" that has emerged on the scene to lead the body towards the promise at such a crucial time as now. Pastor Gary Hawkins, Sr. has placed his anointed pen on the pulse of today's need for spiritual enlightenment in this powerful and poignant message, "Fighting For Your Destiny." I assure you that we will be stronger as a body as we travel across the wilderness of transition into the promised land of Kingdom joy and peace if we use this powerful work as a means of measure and direction. "Let's get ready to rumble!!!!!"

Matthew M. Odum, Sr.,
Pastor, The Temple of Glory Community Church,
Savannah, Georgia

"FIGHTING FOR YOUR DESTINY will encourage you to listen to the voice of the Lord for direction in your life so that you can fulfill the vision that God has for you. Each chapter is filled with profound clarity and life experiences from Pastor Gary Hawkins, Sr. I personally believe this book will benefit Pastors, businessmen, and/or anyone in a leadership position."

Robert Ford,
President, Majestic Media Solutions, Inc.,
Atlanta, Georgia

"In this book Pastor Gary Hawkins, Sr. is giving strong directions for the believer to understand their covenant inheritance. Through this book he helps the believer understand that his reality has to line up with his dreams."

Stanley Calloway,
Pastor, New Fellowship of Praise Community Baptist Church,
Atlanta, Georgia

"If there is anyone in this country that understands destiny it is my brother, Gary Hawkins, Sr. His ministry and life are an example of a man who is serious about doing what God has called him to do, being where God wants him to be, and doing what God wants him to do, at the time God wants him to do it. His heart's desire is to fight until God's will for his life is realized. Read this book if you are serious about fulfilling God's sovereign will for your life. Be Blessed!"

Dwayne Pickett,
Pastor, New Jerusalem Baptist Church,
Jackson, Mississippi

"Champions are valiant fighters who never give up. As with Job, they walk by faith no matter the circumstances. Gary Hawkins, Sr. is one of God's great warriors. In "Fighting For Your Destiny," Pastor Hawkins shares biblical principles and personal challenges that will teach you how to get what God has for you. As business owners, we have applied those teachings and watched our blessings flow. Our business moved from a basement operation to one that now has offices at a major mall in DeKalb County, Georgia. My wife and I continue to walk boldly by faith in the fight for our destiny."

Glenn and Valerie Morgan,
Publishers, On Common Ground News,
DeKalb County, Georgia

"Fighting for your destiny is a vital tool for the cutting edge believer. With the many obstacles that we must face it's good to know the faithfulness of God. Gary Hawkins, Sr. reveals awesome truths that when learned can cause all to experience God's supernatural favor in their lives. I highly recommend this as must reading for those who are determined to have God's best for their lives."

Raymond W. Johnson,
Pastor, Living Faith Christian Center,
Baton Rouge, Louisiana

"God gave Israel 300,000 square miles of land (Joshua 1:4) and the most they ever claimed was 30,000 square miles. They took possession of about one-tenth of what God had given them. Pastor Gary Hawkins, Sr. in his book, "Fighting For Your Destiny" will challenge every church, regardless of size to possess what belongs to them. It is my prayer that thousands of pastors, staff members, Sunday school teachers, and small group leaders will read this book. Somebody once said, "Minds are like parachutes; they work best when they are open." That's the way to read this book!"

Getties Jackson, Sr.,
Pastor, United Christian Ministries,
Greer, South Carolina

"Fighting for Your Destiny is one of the most inspirational and uplifting books for all leaders of tomorrow. I found it to be a road map for success. The application that Pastor Gary Hawkins, Sr. used in his daily walk, during his endurance to build his congregation, will motivate pastors as well as business leaders to learn how to roll with the punches. As a business leader, it has taught me that you cannot be afraid of failing. You must deal with the adversities, surround yourself with positive people, and know that God has ordained your step. Be prepared, this book will take you to the next level of life!"

Robert L. Brown,
President, 100 Black Men of America, Inc.,
DeKalb County, Georgia

"Fighting for your destiny will give you a new perspective regarding the divine mandate on your life. Pastor Gary Hawkins, Sr. has penned, under the unction of the Holy Spirit, a blueprint by which the reader may navigate through the uncertainties of one's future. The practical examples, frank discussions and easy flow of this book make it a must read for those on their way to the ultimate purpose of God for their lives."

Dr. Judith Christie McAllister,
National Recording Artist, Judah Music, Inc.,
Los Angeles, California

"The road to success, (your destiny) is always under construction. It is continually being torn down and built up until it becomes what the Engineer planned for it to be before the foundation of the world. Pastor Gary Hawkins, Sr. not only tells us about the bumps, detours and delays we will experience on our way to fulfilling our destiny, but he shows us how to navigate through them. So put on your seat belt and get ready to get to your spot. It will be adventurous, but enjoy it. It is worth the fight."

Charles E. Wallace,
Pastor, Oasis Christian Church,
Baton Rouge, Louisiana

"God is truly a rewarder of those who diligently seek after him (Hebrews 11:6). If you ever meet a man that diligently seeks and obeys God's plan, knows his assignment for ministry, that relentlessly pursues God's purpose for his life and walks by unyielding faith in God's promises. You have just met one of God's anointed leaders named Pastor Gary Hawkins, Sr. In reading this dynamic book "Fighting For Your Destiny", you will become inspired to fight for what God has prepared for you. And start to live what the Word says in the Bible in Job 36:11, "If they obey and serve Him, they shall spend their days in prosperity and their years in pleasures."

Al B. Sermon,
Pastor, Nothing But The Word Christian Church,
Conyers, Georgia

"I know of no one more qualified to write what I would describe as the best textbook on the subject "Destiny." A book that anyone who wants to be thoroughly informed and inspired about fighting for your destiny today should read and digest."

Rickey T. Washington,
Pastor, Higher Ground Outreach Ministries,
Baton Rouge, Louisiana

"Just as in every mall there is a mall directory, which helps you identify your exact location and your potential destination, "Fighting For Your Destiny" is the motivational map you need to help you get from your present location to your ordained destination!"

Charles Jenkins,
Pastor, Fellowship Missionary Baptist Church,
Chicago, Illinois

"In this exciting book, Fighting For Your Destiny, Pastor Gary Hawkins, Sr. presents eight basic rules for a Christian journey and does it remarkably well. Pastor Hawkins speaks from experience and his wise counsel will help every person achieve greater success in their daily lives. We say that this is the most readable, most constructive and most useful instrument for the teaching of God's Word. This book will influence countless lives."

Gregory and Betty Levett,
Owners, Gregory B. Levett and Sons Funeral Home, Inc.,
DeKalb County, Georgia

"I have been blessed to travel across the world as Bishop Eddie L. Long's armor bearer witnessing God's hand upon great men and women doing phenomenal work for Jesus Christ. Pastor Gary Hawkins, Sr. is a rarity in the body of Christ. His detail to attention, humble spirit, and submissiveness to God has leapfrogged his ministry on the national scene. If you have not heard about him, you will soon! In his book, "Fighting For Your Destiny", Pastor Hawkins has shared kingdom principles to explode your ministry!"

Monte Campbell,
Armor Bearer, New Birth Missionary Baptist Church,
Lithonia, Georgia

"God has given you a great gift (Go In Faith Today) to pursue your destiny. Pastor Gary Hawkins, Sr. has written a masterpiece of a book for those who are seeking to go to the next level."

Thomas Ashford,
Pastor, New Jerusalem Missionary Baptist Church,
East Point, Georgia

In life you run across many acquaintances, and very few that you can call a true friend. My true friend, Pastor Gary Hawkins, Sr. has allowed God to use him in a powerful and miraculous way to step out of all normality's and is crazy enough and radical enough to believe that God will do just what he says. I am amazed at how God has used Pastor Hawkins to witness to others, lessons on kingdom building. It is quite evident to achieve such goals and to speak with such wisdom; Pastor Hawkins has spent time with the master, and is receiving and carrying out the task that God has set before him. I am elated that my friend is bold enough to be real, and real enough to tell others about the goodness of the Lord. Fighting For Your Destiny is a must read!

Mark and Letecia Miles,
Owners, Miles Photography Studio,
Baton Rouge, Louisiana

Fighting for Your DESTINY

Fighting for Your
DESTINY

**Be Strong
and of Good Courage**

GARY HAWKINS, SR.

NILES, ILLINOIS

Copyright © 2003 Gary Hawkins, Sr.
First Edition

Printed in the United States of America

Published by:
Mall Publishing Company
5731 West Howard Street
Niles, Illinois 60714
877.203.2453

Cover Design by Andrew Ostrowski

Book Design by Marlon B. Villadiego

All rights reserved. No part of this book may be reproduced or transmitted in any form or by any means, graphic, electronic, or mechanical, including photocopying, recording, taping, or by any information storage or retrieval system, without the permission in writing from the publisher.

Unless otherwise noted, all scripture quotations are from the King James Version (KJV) of the Holy Bible.

ISBN 0-9741022-8-8

For licensing / copyright information, for additional copies or for use in specialized settings contact:

Gary Hawkins Ministries
P.O. Box 870989
Stone Mountain, Georgia 30087
770.498.5850
Email: vof@voicesfaith.org

DEDICATION

This book is dedicated to God who gave me the vision. I am especially grateful to my pastoral staff who exemplify soldiers equipped for battle. They are battle tested. Each one of these awesome warriors of God has caught the vision allowing me to continue to fight without strongholds.

This book is also dedicated to saints everywhere fighting to take over the possessions God promised.

I am also dedicating this book to my wife, and partner in ministry, Debbie E. Hawkins. Through her love and commitment she has joined me in kingdom work for God. This book is also dedicated to my four children, Elaina, Ashley, Gary, Jr., and Kalen. Thank you for your patience and love.

Finally, this book is dedicated to my mother, Mary Louise Robertson and my mother-n-love, Elzina Owens. Thank you for keeping my head held high, shoulders straight and feet planted firmly to the ground. I am extremely humbled by the dedicated souls God has placed in and around my life.

TABLE OF CONTENTS

Dedication..XI

Table of Contents...XIII

Acknowledgments..XV

Foreword...XIX

Introduction..XXI

Chapter One..1
Fighting For Your Destiny

Chapter Two..15
Rolling With The Punches

Chapter Three..25
A Soldier's Mindset

Chapter Four..39
Holding On To The Promises

Chapter Five...51
Formed To Be Fearless

Chapter Six...63
Failure Is Not Your Final Destination

Chapter Seven..75
Discovering Our Circle of Strength

Chapter Eight...89
Walking In Victory

Conclusion...101

Bibliography..105

ACKNOWLEDGEMENTS

To my best friend in the whole wide world, Debbie Elaine Hawkins, you complete me! I am lost without you in my life! Thank you for being my compass, pointing me in the right directions when I get sidetracked. Thank you for trusting me and pushing me into the next dimension.

To my four wonderful children; Elaina, Ashley, Gary, Jr., and Kalen, I need you to survive! Thank you for unselfishly sharing me with others. It is your love and understanding that keeps me Fighting For My Destiny!

To my mom, Mary Louise Robertson, thank you for preparing me for this level of ministry! Thank you for feeding me nuggets to keep me encouraged and to strengthen me for the journey. Because of you, I am now able to eat the entire chicken. I can now face life's challenges head on.

To my mother-n-love, Elzina Owens, thank you for accepting me into the family. Thank you for never treating me like a son-n-law, but like your own son you give unconditional love to.

To my spiritual father, Bishop Eddie L. Long, thank you for demonstrating your faith by your actions. You have stretched me to believe I can do the impossible through God.

Glenn and Valerie Morgan, you are the greatest! Thank you for always being there for me; this time is no exception. Mae and Alfred Jones, thank you for being my friends. I sleep better at night knowing you are on my side. To Gregory and Betty Levett, your wisdom and love has stretched Debbie and me beyond our wildest imagination.

Special acknowledgment and gratitude goes to Valerie Murkison without whom this book never would have been completed. She pushed her computer to the limit getting pertinent information needed to make this book a success.

Angia Levels and Loraine Dykes were awesome! They were more than just editors to me. They sparked ideas, edited, and encouraged me to stay focus on the divine assignment from God.

To my brother and sister-n-love, Aaron and Mia Hawkins, thank you for leading the way. Your love and commitment to each other continues to demonstrate to others the Christ that rest inside of you.

To the rest of my family, Walter, John, Reginald, Denita, Wayne, Aldreamer, Mary, Warren, Victorina, Chris, Theresa, Gladys, Ann, Gail, Shelia, Dwight, Andrea, Michael, Roy, and Judy, God could not have sent a more loving family. There is not a day that passes by; you are not on my mine. I often pray for your safety as well as prosperity in your life.

To Earl, Jasper, Paula, Tyrone, and Theresa thank you for accepting me just as I am. I am always praying for you that God open up windows and pour you out blessings that you cannot contain.

To my nieces, nephews, cousins, and friends, too many to name, you know I love you and appreciate your love and prayers!

To my pastoral staff, Barbara Jones, Quiana Rosemond, Althea Brooks, Christopher and Leslie Lewis, LaKisha Chatman, Cassandra Clay, Kathleen Dunning, and David Ferebee, I would not trade you with any ministry in the world. Thank you for bringing your "A" game every single day. You are the reason our ministry walks in a spirit of excellence.

Finally, this book was written for saints struggling to possess their land. My desire is that you stir up the gifts God placed inside of you and began FIGHTING FOR YOUR DESTINY!

FOREWORD

Imagine the worst day of your life: Heap on a three-mile run, a hundred push-ups, and a climb up a 50-foot rope. Take away a good-night's sleep, a decent meal, all your hair has been cut off, covered in mud, sweat on your brow, and tears of exhaustion. If you can roll all of that in a 24-hour period, and repeat the process everyday for a number of grueling weeks, then you are ready for boot camp. Boot camp is a place for training soldiers in the art of war. My son, Pastor Gary Hawkins, Sr. prepares us to FIGHT FOR OUR DESTINY by training soldiers for spiritual warfare.

God is looking for soldiers who are willing to sacrifice their own personal agenda for the kingdom. Our destiny lies in the battle. It is God's job to fight our battles, but we must position ourselves and get down to the battlefield. We must eliminate and minimize casualties of war. Major General Donald Rosenblum, a retired Army officer who once commanded the 24th Infantry Division at Fort Stewart said, "Desert Storm casualty estimates were around 100,000 before the war started. The U.S. only lost 146 in combat." As long as we refused to fight the enemy, casualties will continue to pile up in our lives. Satan does not enjoy warfare; his desire is to ambush your ambitions.

In *Fighting For Your Destiny*, Gary Hawkins, Sr. equips us with the necessary tools for success. Through his own demonstration of warfare in the success of his ministry, he understands the make-up of a soldier. A soldier expects warfare. He anticipates a fight. He is equipped and prepared at a moments notice for war. I am not here to take sides; I am here to take over. I am fighting for my destiny!

As you continue to read, I beseech you to put on your spiritual gear for warfare. The battleground is full of surprises and setbacks. Having a soldier's mindset is the proper remedy needed to fight for your destiny!

Bishop Eddie L. Long, D.D., D.H.L.,
Pastor, New Birth Missionary Baptist Church,
Lithonia, Georgia

INTRODUCTION

This book was written in 30 days. This book was inspired by God. On September 1, 2003 I entered into a covenant with God to complete this book by September 30, 2003. The number 30 means maturity. Maturity is synonymous with perfection. Jesus began His ministry at age thirty. David was thirty years old when he reigned as king over Israel. God spoke to me one night while meditating on His Word about writing a book for saints who were struggling to reach their destiny. I made a vow with God that I would complete His book within 30 days. Solomon says in **Ecclesiastes 5:5**, *"Better is it that thou shouldest not vow, than that thou shouldest vow and not pay."*

Over the next 30 days, I canceled appointments and sacrificed family time. I spent more than 10 hours a day writing this book. I was on a divine appointment by God. One day while writing *Fighting For Your Destiny*, a friend called. I told her I was on a divine assignment by God to finish His book within 30 days. She said what I was attempting to do could not be done! She said, "Pastor Hawkins, it takes between 6 months to 3 years to write a book. What you are attempting to do is impossible." I was immediately given a measuring stick of success. I did not know what I was attempting to do, could not be done. I was immediately trapped in a box. I was now operating on someone else's measuring stick of success. As long as I did not know what I was attempting to do could <u>not</u> be done, God was allowing the anointing to flow and my hands to write as He instructed me. As soon as I started measuring my success with someone else's opinion, I stopped writing and the anointing oil stopped flowing. I fell off the horse. My wife, Debbie encouraged me to get back on and fight for my destiny!

God is searching for people like the characters found in this book who are pursuing the things of God that don't know it <u>cannot</u> be done. They have not been given a measuring stick of success. Success is determined by their obedience to God. These people are not leaning to their own understanding. They simply trust God and take Him literally at His Word.

I pray through the reading of this refreshing book, you are pushed into warfare. Your race has already been won, your ship has already come in, and your flight has already landed. Your job is to FIGHT FOR YOUR DESTINY! "Be strong and of a good courage."

1
FIGHTING FOR YOUR DESTINY

I am constantly in awe of God. God has a unique, yet simplistic way of revealing Himself to us and through us. God allows you to see your destiny, tread upon the land, and even taste the fruit thereof. Yet, after showing you your success and revealing to you your destiny God says, "Be strong and of a good courage." In other words, to achieve greatness and become what God intended for you to be, you will have to fight for your destiny. God demonstrated this with Joshua. **Joshua 1:3** says, *"Every place that the sole of your foot shall tread upon, that have I given unto you, as I said unto Moses."* God revealed to Joshua his destiny and the plan that He had for Joshua's life. Notice in **Joshua 1:5-6**, *"There shall not any man be* *able to stand before thee all the days of thy life: as I was with Moses, so I will be with thee: I will not fail thee, nor forsake thee. Be strong and of a good courage: for unto this people shalt thou divide for an inheritance the land, which I sware unto their fathers to give them."* I believe one of the most thought-provoking statements God ever said to Mankind, He said to Joshua. "Be strong and of a good courage." Joshua saw the vision, God said He would be with him every step of the way, yet Joshua knew he was not going to achieve the success God had for his life unless he fought for it. God did not promise Joshua that there would not be scars from the fight, He simply said, He would not fail Joshua while in the battle. God wants to know how badly you desire it. He wants to know if you can stay in your lane when the gunfire erupts. Many people are speaking, shouting, praising, and singing unto God that they are on their way to their destiny and don't even realize they have been disqualified for walking in someone else's lane.

On August 21, 1994, my family and I founded Voices of Faith Ministries with only 10 members. Over the next three years, we grew to 250 members. In October 1997, God spoke to me about leaving my job as a financial analyst at Delta Airlines to go full time in the ministry. God was ready for me to take His ministry to the next level. When I shared this awesome vision with my congregation, several ministers and deacons in my church threatened to leave, if I went full time in the ministry. Their rationale behind their decision was simple. They wanted to buy or build a church edifice to hold worship service and not pay my full-time salary believing it would deplete the church's saving account. God spoke in my spirit saying, "No matter who leaves, I alone am the majority." I was obedient and quit my job believing God would be with me every step of the way. I was not worried about who would remain with me. Just knowing God was on my side outweighed anyone that would abandon the ship. I knew at this time I had to surround myself with positive speaking people. Dr. Creflo Dollar, author of "Uprooting The Spirit of Fear" says, "When doubt or fear come knocking at your door, it is vital that you avoid speaking the devil's words. We have seen how dangerous that can be. But simply keeping your mouth closed is not enough. You must generate faith by speaking God's words instead, regardless of the way circumstances look around you." Our membership immediately took a major blow. In a span of 30 days, our membership dropped from 250 members to 30 and 15 of them were children. I knew something great was about to happen because I was in a fight for my life. You must be willing to die for what God says you're supposed to have. If you are not willing to put everything on the line, then you need to question whether God called

> **You must be willing to die for what God says you're supposed to have.**

you to be what He said you are ordained to be. When you don't have the tenacity, boldness, and the courage to die for what you believe in then it wasn't a vision from God. If God told you to start a business, then you have to suffer through the difficult times until God begins to grow the business. If God instructed you to further your education or placed you on a job that you are currently struggling in, you have to go through the process to reach your destiny. You can't have a vision without problems. Satan's job is to prevent you from reaching your destination. Satan tries to bully you out of your lane. He threatens and pushes you around, because he knows you are not going to fight back. Satan discourages you with harmful words to zap your self-confidence. He even discredits your character to make you feel you don't belong on the playing field. Satan's job is to knock you off course. But if you ever stop allowing the devil to push and kick you around, your destiny is closer than you think. If you ever start giving Satan some left jabs, some upper cuts, and some rope-a-dopes, he will flee from you. Satan needs to hear you say, "I'm coming back off the ropes swinging, you had me down and you may even have staggered me for a second, but baby I'm coming back bigger and meaner than ever. I'm in it for the long run and I'm coming to win today."

Too many are being knocked out for the count. Smelling salt can't even revitalize you. Our job is to take Satan out before he takes us out. Satan knows he can mess with you, but if you ever stand your ground and fight for your destiny, the devil will flee. **James 4:7** says, *"Submit yourselves therefore to God. Resist the devil, and he will flee from you."* Too many of you are in church and God is upset with church folk who claim to have great faith, but are scared to fight the devil. You can't demonstrate great faith in God without getting into a fistfight with the enemy. We had 30 faithful members, yet I knew we were in a fight for our lives. Initially, I was somewhat shaken by the change of events, but I had unwavering faith in God. When the dust cleared and I saw who remained committed to the ministry and the vision God gave me, I knew I had to show them the warrior God had placed within me.

Five days a week, I would rise early in the morning searching for land to build our church. It did not matter to me that we only had 15 adults. I was holding on to the promises of God. I literally took God at His Word. I told my congregation I did not know how God was going to provide, but God was going to prompt someone to bless us with enough money to build His church. The cost of our project was $750,000. The bank gave us 90 days to raise $100,000 as a down payment. We started asking friends and loved ones to contribute toward this momentous task.

I decided to approach the Stone Mountain Association of the Georgia Baptist Convention to inquire about a loan, since we are part of the

Georgia Baptist Convention. The Georgia Baptist Convention provides financial assistance for land purchases to churches that are part of its body. If you purchase 8 acres or more, the convention will lend you $25,000. We were purchasing 20 acres. To make a long story short, I was turned down. The association did not feel we were a financially strong enough church to handle the debt. I understood their reasoning, but God's hand was on me for a greater work. I was fighting for my destiny. I resigned from the association. I knew if our church was going to get to the next level and march toward the destination God ordained, I had to rid myself of any negative vibes.

Two weeks earlier, I was up at 2:00 a.m. studying the blueprint of our future church when the Holy Spirit spoke to me: "Gary, open the yellow pages and call this church and make an appointment with the pastor." Later that morning, I called the church and made the appointment with the pastor. I knew absolutely nothing about the church. I was obedient to God.

Two weeks later, I received a phone call from the church secretary reminding me of my appointment the next morning with the pastor I was meeting. I asked for directions because I had no idea where I was going or who I was meeting. I was just being obedient to God. The pastor and I enjoyed a wonderful lunch together. I shared the vision God gave me and poured out my heart to him concerning ministry. He asked, "Gary, have you ever thought about joining the Georgia Baptist Convention?" In my mind, I said, "Lord, you brought me out here to get insulted again!" I explained that they had recently turned me down for a loan of $25,000 and I was no longer associated with the Convention. He picked up his cell phone and called the Georgia Baptist Convention. He said, "I want you to cut a check for $25,000 for my good friend Gary Hawkins, Sr., pastor of Voices of Faith Ministries in Stone Mountain. He is about to do a great work for God." After praising God and regaining my composure, I asked "Who are you to call and get the Georgia Baptist Convention to write a check to us for $25,000?" He said, "You don't know who I am?" I said, "No sir." He said, "I am the president of the Georgia Baptist Convention." His name is Dr. Frank Cox, pastor of North Metro Baptist Church, one of the largest churches in the state of Georgia. We were immediately encouraged by Rev. Sid Hopkins, Executive Director of the Gwinnett Metro Baptist Association to join their association. Joining their association has been one of the best moves our church has made. Sid has been an awesome role model for helping churches to grow. The Georgia Baptist Convention asked the Gwinnett Metro Baptist Association to write the check for $25,000 to us.

Our church launched a letter-writing campaign to tell friends, loved ones and others all over the United States of the work we were doing. The money began to pour in to bless the work of God. Two of the first people to respond were celebrities:

Actor Blair Underwood and Todd Kinchens, former Atlanta Falcons Wide Receiver. I remember getting a letter from Todd Kinchens saying, "Pastor Hawkins, when I looked into your eyes and saw the picture of your family, I knew God was about to do a great work in your life." Needless to say, when the dust cleared, $103,000 was collected in 90 days. Praise God! Don't be afraid to dream! John Maxwell, author of "Failing Forward" said, "To achieve your dreams, you must embrace adversity and make failure a regular part of your life. If you're not failing, you're probably not really moving forward." Don't be afraid to fight for your destiny!

> **God doesn't want wimps in the body of Christ.**

God doesn't want wimps in the body of Christ. He is looking for warriors who are not afraid to die for what they believe in. One of the most fascinating characters in the bible is Jonathan. He was a man of faith. He believed the Lord could save them from the Philistines regardless of how many there were and how few were with him. Jonathan's father, King Saul was a coward living in fear. It is extremely important to have the right people around you when fighting for your destiny. **1 Samuel 14:6-7** says, *"And Jonathan said to the young man that bare his armour, Come, and let us go over unto the garrison of these uncircumcised: it may be that the LORD will work for us: for there is no restraint to the LORD to save by many or by few. And his armourbearer said unto him, Do all that is* *in thine heart: turn thee; behold, I am with thee according to thy heart."*

Jonathan had a man of faith for his armorbearer, one willing to go with his master in any venture. Jonathan did not hope the war ended. He believed through faith, he and his armorbearer alone could defeat the Philistines. Dr. Fred Price, author of "How Faith Works" says, "Hope has no substance to it. Hope is a dream. Hope is just an idle thought. It has no tangibility. Substance means that which has materiality. Hope has none. "I hope some day to be rich." That has no tangibility. It's just a dream, just a figment of my mind. What faith does is give hope substance. Faith gives hope materiality. Faith gives hope tangibility. Faith gives hope substance."

Gideon was another man who God used for a mighty work. He had just finished assembling 32,000 soldiers to fight against the Midianites. But God was not pleased with the number of men assembled. He told Gideon to proclaim to the people whoever is fearful and afraid, let him return home. God's rationale was simple; He wanted you to know that the victory was not in the numbers, but in trusting in Him alone. Twenty-two thousand went home leaving 10,000 men who were ready to die fighting for their destiny. Yet there were still too many men assembled for God to get the glory. **Judges 7:5-6** says, *"So he brought down the people unto the water: and the LORD said unto Gideon, Every one that lappeth of the water with his tongue, as a dog lappeth, him shalt thou set by him-*

self; likewise every one that boweth down upon his knees to drink. And the number of them that lapped, putting their hand to their mouth, were three hundred men: but all the rest of the people bowed down upon their knees to drink water." God told Gideon; by the 300 men that lapped like a dog will I save you and deliver the enemy into your hands. God is looking for men and women of war who has the unction to take God at His Word. God has given us the power to overcome all obstacles. God made us a promise in Leviticus 26:8 that five people shall chase a 100 away and 100 would be able to put 10,000 to flight. In other words, Gideon's 300 men could have defeated 300,000 to 1,500,000 warriors. God is looking for men and women who come armed with their boxing gloves on ready to do battle.

> **A church is a spiritual boot camp.**

If we expect to reach our destiny, our mindset has to change. Paul understood this concept. Paul says in **I Corinthians 9:26-27**, *"I therefore so run, not as uncertainly; so fight I, not as one that beateth the air: But I keep under my body, and bring it into subjection: lest that by any means, when I have preached to others, I myself should be a castaway."*

The Greek word hupopiazo means "keep under my body." This simply means to strike one under the eye; to beat black and blue. Paul says I die daily. Every morning I wake up I beat myself up. Paul understood that he could not have his body rule over his mind. We must enlist ourselves into a local church. A church is a spiritual boot camp. Boot camp is where you go for instructions on how to fight warfare. It's where training takes place. A church is where you get hand-to-hand combat instructions on how to defeat the devil. A soldier's mindset must be different than civilians. II **Timothy 2:3-4** says, *"Thou therefore endure hardness, as a good soldier of Jesus Christ. No man that warreth entangleth himself with the affairs of this life; that he may please him who hath chosen him to be a soldier."* A soldier doesn't hang out with civilians unless he is recruiting them. A soldier is at all time equipped and ready for battle. We must put on the whole armour of God. We are in a constant battle with Satan and he is not fighting us with flesh and blood. **Ephesians 6:12** says, *"For we wrestle not against flesh and blood, but against principalities, against powers, against the rulers of the darkness of this world, against spiritual wickedness in high places."* He is using trickery to pull us down. I'm just your instructor. My job is to give you the guidelines and the principles to know how to fight the devil. You cannot fight the devil the way you use to. He's too cunning and deceptive.

One of the most intriguing characters in the bible is the persistent widow found in Luke 18. The persistent widow understood if she was going to avenge her adversary, it would come through her fighting for her life. She did this through pestering the unjust judge. She repeatedly came, pestering the judge beyond endurance, which was the secret of her success in getting an answer. The judge did not fear God nor regard man, but after he tolerated her pestering to the breaking point, he concluded that he would never have any more peace until he got rid of her; the only way to do this was by granting her request. Notice in **Luke 18:5**, *"Yet because this widow troubleth me, I will avenge her, lest by her continual coming she weary me."* Weary is the same word in the Greek as **hupopiaza,** which means to hit under the eye; to blacken the eye; to beat black and blue. The unjust judge was exhausted from the spiritual beating of the persistent widow. She knew what it would take to reach her destiny. Dr. Martin Luther King, Jr. was a visionary. He once said, "A man who has nothing he would die for, is not fit to live." You have to fight for what you believe in to make it happen.

God gave us a road map for success through His communication with Joshua. In Joshua 1:1-18, God reminded Joshua to "Be strong and of a good courage" four times. God again stressed to Joshua the land, house, and fruit is yours, but the only way you will become successful is through fighting for your destiny. The people in the city have to know you are a man of faith who fights for what is promised. Pastor Kim and his wife, Elder Valerie Brown, friends of mine from Chesapeake, Virginia tell the story of some property next to their church they needed for parking. They approached the owner inquiring about renting his property for parking and the owner turned them down. The owner told Pastor Kim Brown his reputation preceded him. He told him he had a reputation in the city. Pastor Brown asked, "What does that mean?" The owner said, "If I rent you this property, before I know it, you would try to own it." The city knows Pastor Brown as a man who fights for what God promises. Oh by the way, his church now owns the property. They are using the house on the property to allow one of their church members to live there. Praise the Lord!

CHAPTER 1
FOR DISCUSSION

1. Why does God tell Joshua "Be strong and of a good courage?"

2. Why is it important to fight for your destiny?

3. Do you feel adversity when pursuing your goals?

4. Why is it important to change our mindset when reaching our destiny?

5. Why doesn't a soldier hang out with civilians?

6. What tactics did the persistent widow use to get the unjust judge to avenge her adversaries?

7. What is the definition of the Greek word, "hupopiaza"?

2
ROLLING WITH THE PUNCHES

In order to reach your destiny, you must make some adjustments along the way. It is impossible to be in a fight for any length of time without being hit by an opponent. It does not matter how clever you may be or how strong you think you are, your opponent will eventually land a punch. We have to learn to roll with the punches. Some punches are going to penetrate the best of defenses. A boxing trainer puts grease on a fighter's face to avoid a direct hit

Some punches are going to penetrate the best of defenses.

from his opponent. Oftentimes, fighters are knocked out because of direct hits. A good boxer knows he has to develop great defense skills to avoid a direct blow. Satan operates in a similar fashion. Satan's mission is to give you a Technical Knock-Out (TKO). He is equipped to kill, steal, and destroy. Satan is known for throwing sucker punches. A sucker punch is when someone hits you without warning. Your assignment is to learn the art of self-defense by rolling with the punches as they are being thrown. You must be able to see the enemy coming.

Heavyweight champion Mike Tyson was one of the most feared boxers on the face of the earth. In his prime, opponents lasted three rounds or less. He was known as a knockout artist. No fighter could go the distance with him. Tyson's nickname was "Iron-Mike." In many people's eyes, he was absolutely unstoppable.

> **Satan does not want to get into a fist fight with you.**

On one ordinary night in 1990, an unknown fighter by the name of James "Buster" Douglass was his next challenger. Buster scored one of the biggest upsets in boxing history knocking Tyson out in 10 rounds. What happened? Tyson was not use to anyone standing up to him. He was not use to his opponents fighting back. In every round Buster Douglass became stronger, Tyson grew weaker. Tyson was not comfortable with another fighter being more aggressive than he. Satan has these same qualities. He enjoys being the aggressor. The devil thrives on being the bully on the block. **1 Peter 5:8** says, *"Be sober, be vigilant; because your adversary the devil, as a roaring lion, walketh about,* *seeking whom he may devour."* Satan does not want to get into a fist fight with you. He realizes the longer you tangle with him, the better chances you have of being victorious. Satan doesn't want to get in a wrestling match; he just wants to throw a sucker punch. He doesn't enjoy fighting with those who fight back. The next upper cut the devil throws your way trying to prevent you from moving into your destiny, roll with the punch and deliver a blow of your own.

Knowing your purpose will help you better roll with the punches when the enemy tries to sidetrack you from your destiny. Once a month, I visit a popular restaurant in Decatur, Georgia known for its soul food. The food is excellent, but the servers' attitudes are horrible. I am asked quite often by my staff, "Why do you continually eat at this restaurant knowing customer service is bad?" I know my purpose for patronizing their business. Every time I visit the restaurant, I see the punch coming. I don't dine at this restaurant because of bad customer service. I eat there frequently because of what I desire. I desire their food. I love their collard greens, baked chicken, macaroni and cheese, peach cobbler, just to name a few. Because I know my purpose for going, it is easier for me to roll with the punches.

There will be people in your life who try to justify your successes. Four years ago, Voices of Faith had 75 members. Today, approximately 4,000 are on roll. Pastors and preachers have visited our ministry from all over the country. They have given many reasons for the success of our ministry. One pastor mentioned our success is due to our location. Another said our fast growth is due to an influx of new homes built in the area. One pastor even mentioned our demographics in the south being the leading cause of our growth. I've learned to roll with the punches. I know our phenomenal growth is due to God's grace and mercy! We are not the only church in the community. There are thousands of other churches in the South that are not growing. When people approach you with negative remarks, roll with the punches and reflect your success to God alone.

One of my heroes in the bible who demonstrates the art of rolling with the punches is the Canaanite woman in Matthew 15. She understood her purpose and was determined not to allow anything or anyone to stop her from being successful. Her desire and purpose was to see her daughter delivered from being demon possessed. She approaches Jesus with a request of healing, but He ignores her. The Canaanite woman then proceeds to worship Christ even though He has not answered her request. Finally, Jesus responds by calling the woman a dog. **Matthew 15:26-27** says, *"But he answered and said, It is not meet to take the children's bread, and to cast it to dogs. And she said, Truth, Lord: yet the dogs eat of the crumbs which fall from their masters' table."* It was her response that caught Jesus' attention. God's anointing is so powerful; the

Canaanite woman knew her daughter could get healed off God's leftovers. The Canaanite woman was willing to be ridiculed for the sake of seeing her daughter healed. She understood her purpose. The Canaanite woman acknowledged her position as undeserving and without legal covenant rights to the children's bread, yet she used the Lord's own words concerning dogs as grounds for further claim for healing. Even dogs have some rights—rights to the crumbs that the master throws away and would give to them. Jesus Christ could not turn down such faith based upon such claims. Because of her great faith, Jesus healed her daughter that very hour. Her faith was connected with her persistence and the ability to roll with the punches during adversity. God oftentimes wants to see how bad you desire it. You've asked God for healing, deliverance, and even to fix your marriage. Yet, God has ignored your prayer request. You've become frustrated from the lack of results. This is God's way of testing your will and endurance. Rolling with the punches will help you develop greater results with God.

> **Rolling with the punches has become a mainstay of mine.**

Rolling with the punches has become a mainstay of mine. I believe in the concept. I possess the skills. I have experienced the fruit of my labor because of this godly principle. I use it every time I need something desperate from God that would glorify Him. In 2001, we were in desperate need of a new place to worship due to overcrowding in our current church edifice. God was growing our church at an astonishing rate. Our current church building could only seat 400. We had three morning worship services beginning at 7:00 a.m., 9:00 a.m., and 11:00 a.m. At one time, we were turning away approximately 40 cars a Sunday because of the lack of parking and seating capacity in the church. I knew it was time to build a new church edifice for God. We had drawn up blueprints of a 40,000-square-foot Family Life Center. The 1,600 seat center includes a full size basketball court; a bookstore; an aerobic room, weight room, men's and women's saunas, kitchen, banquet room and a kid's zone. The cost of the project was $3,000,000. I approached the bank about financing the loan, but was denied. I had become a master of rolling with the punches. I refused to take no for an answer. I had so much faith in God; I gave permission to the construction company to break ground on the property, even though we had no loan approved. Our congregation held a ground breaking ceremony on the property. Bulldozers and other tractors began to arrive on the church grounds. Trees were being knocked down; the foundation of the new building was quickly taking shape. Yet, we could not find any bank to finance the loan. I was trusting God through my demonstration of faith. I knew if we were to succeed in getting a loan to build this building for God's glory, I had to continue to roll with the punches even though I did not have all the answers. Finally, a local bank agreed to finance the loan. Voices of Faith had a victory celebration because of God's answered prayer. Several weeks into the building project, we ran into some unexpected snares. The property we were attempting to build the Family Life Center upon was considered by Gwinnett County and Sparks-Grizzard Construction Company as "bad dirt." It cost the church an additional $100,000 to bring in good dirt unto the property. The bank called our church and Sparks-Grizzard into a meeting to discuss possibly canceling the project. God was giving me another opportunity to roll with the punches. David Sparks, owner of Sparks-Grizzard said, "I believe in Pastor Gary Hawkins, Sr. If you decide to cancel the project, we will continue to build this church edifice knowing God would provide." Even after the building was finished, we still had not closed on the loan for the church. June 18-21, 2002, we dedicated the church building believing God would provide. World renowned speakers such as my spiritual father, Bishop Eddie L. Long of New Birth Missionary Baptist Church in Lithonia, Georgia consecrated the building. Other speakers who participated in the week long celebration included: Bishop Dale Bronner of Word of Faith Family Worship Center in Austell, Georgia, Pastor Leroy Woodard of Christian Rescue Mission Church in Houston, Texas, and Pastor Wiley Jackson of Gospel

> **God did not promise you that your journey would be easy.**

Tabernacle in Atlanta, Georgia. Three weeks of worshipping God in the building, we still had not closed on the loan. I was still rolling with the punches. One day as I was driving to church, I received a call on my cell phone from the loan officer of the bank congratulating us on the approval of our new loan. Praise the Lord! God did not promise you that your journey would be easy; therefore it is imperative that you develop the mindset to roll with the punches until your breakthrough occurs. We must surround ourselves with people who are warriors for God. We must mimic their behavior patterns. John Maxwell, author of "Running With The Giants" says, "David, perhaps more than anyone else in the stadium, is the person I most want to run a lap with. I watch him as he approaches us. He is dressed as a king in colorful robes with a jeweled sword on his hip and a crown on his head, but carries himself like a great warrior—powerful, relaxed yet alert, and poised for any situation." It is important that we connect ourselves with people who are experts in dealing with adversity. We must get hooked up with people who can teach others how to effectively roll with the punches.

> **It is important that we connect ourselves with people who are experts in dealing with adversity.**

CHAPTER 2
FOR DISCUSSION

1. Why are adjustments needed to reach your destiny?

2. What does "Rolling with the Punches" mean?

3. Why is it important to know your purpose when fighting for your destiny?

4. Who are some people in your life trying to justify your success?

5. What was one of the strong attributes the Canaanite woman possessed?

6. What did you learn from this chapter concerning adversity?

7. What must we do until our breakthrough occurs?

3

A SOLDIER'S MINDSET

A soldier's mindset is a must while fighting for your destiny. A soldier's mindset is the spiritual tool needed to advance in the kingdom. Soldiers are trained to be mentally prepared for warfare. They understand the mental challenge it takes to complete their assignment. The first thing happens with a soldier is to get their thought patterns to change. A soldier's mind is emptied of all negative thought patterns such as, fear, failure, procrastination, and laziness just to name a few. Secondly, a soldier's spirit begins a shifting process in preparing him for greatness. There is a renewing of a soldier's spirit. Positive vibes are being spoken in a soldier's spirit. Finally, your body aligns itself with your spirit to accomplish the vision.

I am in constant prayer asking God to give me a soldier's mindset. I recognize if I am going to get to the next level with God, I must be equipped and trained with a soldier's mindset. A soldier will not buck the system. He does not question authority. He does not ask questions such as: "Why and How?" His job is to strictly obey his commander in chief. A soldier is willing and ready to submit to his superior officer.

A soldier will not buck the system.

When a civilian enlists in the military, he immediately reports to boot camp. Boot camp is a place for training soldiers the art of war. When a civilian enters boot camp, he loses his own identity. He is the property of the United States Military. He no longer has control of his own life. A civilian is stripped of his clothing and given special clothing representative of his military unit. He is told to cut his hair and keep a clean shaven face. Time is no longer a factor. He is told when to eat, sleep, and relax. The military's assignment is to deprogram him. If he bucks the system, they court marshal him. He is thrown into the U.S. military prison. They even discharge him from the military by giving him a dishonorable discharge.

A soldier's mindset is critical to your success with God. A Christian must have similar characteristics to advance in the kingdom. The moment you accepted Jesus Christ as Lord and the head of your life, you entered into a spiritual boot camp. In this boot camp, you were purchased with a price. Jesus gave His life so that you may enter into a covenant with God. Jesus gave you the right to join God's spiritual boot camp. You lose your own identity. You no longer have control over your life. You become the property of the Godhead, the Father, Son, and Holy Spirit. Jesus says in **John 15:4-5**, *"Abide in me, and I in you. As the branch cannot bear fruit of itself, except it abide in the vine; no more can ye, except ye abide in me. I am the vine, ye are the branches: He that abideth in me, and I in him, the same bringeth forth much fruit: for without me ye can do nothing."* A Christian is stripped of his spiritual clothing. His walk is different. His talk now commands authority. A spiritual boot camp is designed to deprogram you of any impurities. If a person refuses to enlist in God's army, he is cast into outer darkness. He is like a branch which has been cut off and withered away. Jesus says in **John 15:6**, *"If a man abide not in me, he is cast forth as a branch, and is withered; and men gather them, and cast them into the fire, and they are burned."* Abiding in Jesus Christ means believing He is God's Son. It means receiving Christ as Savior and Lord. Abiding in Christ also mean to do what God says, continuing in faith, and relating to the community of believers to stay in their lane.

I believe the reason why we have not advanced in the kingdom is due to our weak and fleshly mindset. We have allowed civilians to pour garbage in

> **A Christian is stripped of his spiritual clothing.**

our spirits. We challenge authority. We question their motives. We undermine their decision-making process. We even rip them behind their backs. We are not soldiers for God; we are our own worst enemy. Our job is to never leave our spiritual boot camp. Our spiritual boot camp is where God dwells. Our spiritual boot camp is the Holy of Holies. It is the most intimate and powerful place of God.

How do we shift our minds to get a soldier's mindset? We need to have a renewing of the mind. **Romans 12:2** says, *"And be not conformed to this world: but be ye transformed by the renewing of your mind, that ye may prove what is that good, and acceptable, and perfect, will of God"* Your mind has to get in line with your destiny. If you can conceive in your mind victory, your destiny is only a shout away. If you can see your destiny, God will manifest it in the flesh. It truly is a mind thing. Your mind has to be trained to develop this type of behavior.

> **Our spiritual boot camp is the Holy of Holies.**

In order to develop a soldier's mindset, your environment must change. You can no longer associate with the same people. You must be connected to people that will add value to your life, not zap you of your strength. A soldier recognizes he must fight to get to his destiny. He knows he must endure hardship. A soldier realizes he must have people in his inner circle who speaks the same language as he. **II Timothy 2:3-4** says, *"Thou therefore endure hardness, as a good soldier of Jesus Christ. No man* *that warreth entangleth himself with the affairs of this life; that he may please him who hath chosen him to be a soldier."* Notice, Paul suggests soldiers don't hang out with civilians unless they are recruiting them. Soldiers don't hang out with gossipers. They don't associate with people who will discourage them from reaching their destiny. Civilians will cause you to miss your mark. They will clog up your blessings. Civilians will prevent you from getting your breakthrough. Civilians have a crab-in-the-bucket mentality. If they see you heading to the top, their job is to pull you back in the bucket. They want to keep you where they are and not where God wants you to be. A soldier has responsibility. Notice, what Paul says in II Timothy 2:4? The soldier is working to please the one who has chosen him. God chose us, we did not choose Him. The Lord saw something in you. You weren't worthy of the blessings, but God saw something in you to draw you to Jesus Christ. He chose you to be a soldier, God chose you to enter boldly in the throne room of grace and mercy. Just as the soldier lives up to certain standards if he is a good one, an athlete obeys the rules of the game if he wins, so the Christian must live up to the rules if he expects a crown of glory and eternal fruit. A soldier must be willing to sacrifice to achieve the results he wants. Like soldiers, we have to give up worldly security and endure rigorous discipline to get our destiny. A

> **The soldier is working to please the one who has chosen him.**

soldier expects warfare. He anticipates a fight. He is equipped and prepared at a moments notice for war. He keeps his gear intact. **Ephesians 6:11** says, *"Put on the whole armour of God, that ye may be able to stand against the wiles of the devil."*

As Christians, we battle against "principalities and powers." We battle Satan in the spirit. He is not flesh. Satan is a vicious and cunning fighter. He is constantly thinking of schemes to distract you from achieving greatness with God. To withstand Satan's attacks, we must put on the whole armor of God. We must equip ourselves with the **"Breastplate of righteousness."** The Breastplate of righteousness is God's approval to do business against the devil. We must put on **"Shoes."** Spiritual shoes give us the ability to spread the Gospel of Jesus Christ. A **"Shield"** must be added to defeat the devil. A shield is our faith. It is the gas in our car. It is the food in our body. A shield is the ticking within our clock. A **"Helmet"** is needed to be successful against your enemy. Satan wants to make us doubt God, Jesus, and our salvation. The helmet protects our minds from doubting God's saving work for us. Finally, the most important armor of all is the **"Sword."** The sword is the Word of God. The sword is the only weapon of offense in this list of armor. There are times when we need to take the offense against Satan and his attacks.

One of the most powerful and thought-provoking illustrations on how to gain this military mindset is found in Matthew 8:5-13. A centurion came to Jesus seeking help for his dying soldier. A centurion is a captain of 100 Roman soldiers. This centurion was an unchurched man. He did not have a relationship with God. He was not use to chanting scriptures in the church. He knew nothing about altar calls or singing hymns. The centurion had no prior experience of praise and worship. He did not know the proper protocol to see Jesus. He did not even have an appointment with the Master. The only thing he had going for himself was his ability to submit to authority. He approached Jesus to heal his servant who was in much pain and was dying. Notice, the centurion did not come on his own behalf. He came on the behalf of a helpless soldier. Jesus never questions him. Jesus immediately says, "I will come and heal him." This centurion makes a thought-provoking statement that has affected my life for ever. **Matthew 8:8** says, *"The centurion answered and said, Lord, I am not worthy that thou shouldest come under my roof: but speak the word only, and my servant shall be healed."* The centurion told Jesus to speak the Word only. He understood the power of the tongue. **Proverbs 18:21** says, *"Death and life are in the power of the tongue: and they that love it shall eat the fruit thereof."* The Centurion understood the divine principle of speaking things into existence even though it had yet to be manifested. He expressed to Christ his humbleness. He told Jesus he was not worthy for Him to come to his house. He

> **Most importantly, he understood authority.**

had not lived the life God expected. He was not trying to be something that he was not. He was keeping it real. Most importantly, he understood authority. He was trained to submit to a higher ranking officer. He recognized Jesus as being a more superior rank than he. The centurion called Jesus, "Lord." He knew how to give and receive authority. **Matthew 8:9** says, *"For I am a man under authority, having soldiers under me: and I say to this man, Go, and he goeth; and to another, Come, and he cometh; and to my servant, Do this, and he doeth it."* The centurion was sharing with Christ that he had authority over 100 soldiers. They follow his every command. He recognized that Christ had a higher power than he. He knew Jesus Christ had power and authority over demons. **Matthew 28:18,** *"And Jesus came and spake unto them, saying, All power is given unto me in heaven and in earth."* The centurion had been trained all his life to submit. He knew not to question authority. His success was in his submissiveness. The centurion understood the protocol of authority. The centurion knew if Jesus spoke the "Word" only, his servant would be healed. Jesus marveled at the centurion's faith. Jesus had never met anyone who had demonstrated such great faith. There was no one in the church who walked in that type of faith. There was no one found in Israel with that great of faith. Jesus' disciples did not demonstrate this type of faith. They watched Jesus pray, they saw Him perform miracles, and yet

> **Jesus marveled only twice in the bible.**

did not produce this type of faith at the time of the biblical recording. This was an unchurched soldier who caused Jesus to marvel. He did not attend Sunday school. The centurion never showed up to mid-week worship service. Jesus marveled only twice in the bible. The only other time Jesus marveled was at the saint's unbelief in Mark 6:6. Jesus told the centurion to go on his way; his great faith had healed his servant. His soldier was healed in the same hour.

> **The centurion taught us how to serve.**

Our faith in God must duplicate that of the centurion. We must develop the mindset of a soldier to experience the same success from God. It is our faith that pleases and glorifies God. Developing a soldier's mindset is the key to achieving greatness for Him.

The centurion taught us how to serve. He taught us to have a servant mentality. Jesus was a master at this principle. I am reminded of when Jesus was washing the disciple's feet and Peter did not want Christ to touch his feet. He felt unworthy. Jesus was demonstrating to us how to serve in the kingdom. **John 13:8-9** says, *"Peter saith unto him, Thou shalt never wash my feet. Jesus answered him, If I wash thee not, thou hast no part with me. Simon Peter saith unto him, Lord, not my feet only, but also my hands and my head."* We must develop a servant's mentality to advance in the kingdom of God. The Marriott Hotel understood the concept of servant hood. J.W. Marriott, Jr. author of "The

Spirit to Serve" says, "When employees know that their problems will be taken seriously, that their ideas and insights matter, they're more comfortable and confident. In turn, they're better equipped to deliver their best on the job and to the customer. Everyone wins: the company, the employee, the customer." They breed success through their servant's mentality.

We have yet to master authority. God will test you, before He elevates you to the next level. God will cause you to submit to people in your life who are less qualified for the job than you. Your prosperity is not in your knowledge; it is in your submission. God wants to see can you respect another man's destiny, before He propels you into yours. **Luke 16:10** says, *"He that is faithful in that which is least is faithful also in much: and he that is unjust in the least is unjust also in much."* God pushes you into your destiny, while you assist another man in his.

> **Your prosperity is not in your knowledge; it is in your submission.**

One of the greatest illustrations of submission and respecting authority can be found in Luke 17:11-19. There were ten leprous men standing outside this certain village when they discovered Jesus passing through the village. They recognized Him as a man with all authority. With a loud voice, they began to cry out asking Jesus to heal them. Pay close attention to **Luke 17:13**, *"And they lifted up their voices, and said, Jesus, Master, have mercy on* us." The moment the lepers used the word "Master", they were under submission to Jesus. Their breakthrough and healing was only going to come through obedience. When Jesus saw them, He told them to go and show themselves to the priest. Leprosy was a very contagious disease. The only way lepers were allowed to enter back into the city, the priest had to publicly announce and declare their healing. **Luke 17:14** says, *"And when he saw them, he said unto them, Go show yourselves unto the priests. And it came to pass, that, as they went, they were cleansed."* This is very important; the lepers were not healed because Jesus told them to go to the priest. God often speaks to us, but we refuse to obey. We ignore God and oftentimes do the opposite of what He expects from us. The lepers were healed because they <u>went</u> to the priest. Their healing was not just in hearing Jesus, but obediently doing what He asked them do. We must be both hearers and doers of the Word. Notice, they never questioned Jesus. They never doubted Jesus' Word. There was no confusion or misunderstanding. The communication between Jesus and the ten lepers were clear and concise. They were healed because they trusted in Him who they called "Master".

      We must develop this same type of mindset. We must become like soldiers ready to embrace spiritual warfare. We must recognize God as God.

> **I think like a soldier, walk like a soldier, and I fight like a soldier.**

We must take heed to God's very Word. We must not question God when He speaks to us. We must respond to God's request as if we know He will get the glory for our obedience. We must stand tall in the saddle and let the world know business as usual is unacceptable to attain the prize.

I am a soldier in the army of the Lord. I have a soldier's mindset. I think like a soldier, I walk like a soldier, and I fight like a soldier. I am trained for spiritual combat. I am equipped to take out the devil, and cast out demons. I've been given a license by God to walk in my lane to pursue my destiny. I am anointed to prosper and possess the land. I am obedient, trustworthy, humble, submissive, loyal, and ready to do battle with the enemy. If you fit all these attributes or have a desire to learn how to acquire them, I invite you to accept your responsibility and join The Spiritual Boot Camp of the Lord and do business for the kingdom of God. In the words of my spiritual father, Bishop Eddie L. Long of New Birth, I am not here to take sides; I am here to take over. I am fighting for my destiny. I am fighting to get back what the devil stole. The only way I am going to recover all of my blessings is with a soldier's mindset.

CHAPTER 3
FOR DISCUSSION

1. What does it mean to have a "Soldier's Mindset"?

2. Why does a soldier's mind need deprogramming?

3. What is a "Spiritual Boot Camp"?

4. What are the 5 spiritual weapons of warfare we need to equip ourselves to fight the devil?

5. What is the definition of a "Centurion"?

6. What type of faith we must possess in order to make Jesus marvel?

7. Do you feel a soldier's mindset is needed to reach our destiny?

4
HOLDING ON TO THE PROMISES

Whenever you wait on a promise, it brings great anticipation. Every morning I wake up, I am like the kid in the candy store. I am like the groom on his honeymoon. I am like the postman who has delivered his last mail. I am excited about holding on to the promises of God! I am restless and oftentimes can not sleep. My eating habits have changed. My study habits have increased. The anointing on my life has allowed me to understand God's Word and His promises better. I am a living testimony. God keeps allowing me to pick up nuggets along the roadside to keep me encouraged. I am now waiting on the whole chicken. I want the legs, thighs, wings,

> **I am now waiting on the whole chicken.**

and breast. I am waiting on every promise God made to me. The anticipation of my breakthrough keeps me laughing, shouting, praising, and worshipping God. Every morning God awakens me, I am a day closer to the promise. Every night God causes me to sleep; I am restless until the break of day knowing my destiny is right around the corner. The anticipation alone can make or break you. I have no other option; God must bring to pass what He has allowed me to see in the Spirit. I rejoice when others are achieving success and reaching their destiny. It encourages me to know God is answering prayer and I am next in line. My promise is on the way. It has already been shipped; I am just awaiting its arrival. I am anticipating any day now Federal Express and UPS will knock on my door releasing my package. I can't wait to un-wrap the blessings of God. I am holding on to the promises of God.

> **Every morning God awakens me, I am a day closer to the promise.**

In 1989 while living in San Diego, California, God made a promise to me that I will never forget. The promise changed my life for ever. I began to have a series of dreams over a two-year period. I was having dreams of preaching before thousands of people. God revealed to me that I would pastor a church well over 20,000 members, but not for selfish reasons. It was to impact the world for the glory of God. God is looking for disciples, not pew members. God is searching for spiritual giants in the body of Christ who are ready to take authority for Him. The dreams were terrifying. It was more than I could handle so I would wake myself from the dream. I was not prepared for what God was revealing to me. I was not an eloquent speaker nor was I heavily involved in ministry. As a matter of fact, I was afraid to speak in public. I hated doing presentations on my job before my boss and co-workers. I would dehydrate and break out in a cold sweat during my presentations. Each dream had me speaking before thousands and each time I would awake myself. One night as I was dreaming, God refused to allow me to wake myself. I went to the podium before thousands and said, **"There is a Word!"** And that Word can be found in Matthew 22:14." God immediately wakes me up from the dream. I rose up quickly out of bed and opened up my bible to read **Matthew 22:14**. It read, *"For many are called, but few are chosen."* I knew God was calling me for a greater work. God was calling me to preach the Gospel of Jesus Christ. God showed me a glimpse of what my destiny would look like if I remained faithful and obedient. My destiny and the promises of God are tied to the dream. In order for me to reach my destiny, I must duplicate and manifest exactly what God revealed to me in the dream. Every single time I get up to preach the Word of God, I begin my message by saying, **"There is a Word!"** Each time I say, **"There is a Word!"** I am repeating what was

> **My destiny and the promises of God are tied to the dream.**

revealed to me in the dream and God is bringing me closer to my destiny. The promise God made to me is tied to my dream. Each time I openly pronounced to the congregation, "There is a Word!" God is bringing me closer to the promise of bringing over 20,000 soldiers to Christ. Even though God had revealed to me my destiny, fighting for what God ordained for me to have was the only way to achieve it. I must hold onto the promise of God. God did not say there were not going to be rough roads ahead. But as long as I stay focused on the promises of God, it must come to pass. King David said in Psalms 144:1, *"Blessed be the LORD my strength, which teacheth my hands to war, and my fingers to fight."* God is looking for soldiers who understand that their destiny is already mapped out. All they need to do is walk in their lane and allow the glory of God to shine in their lives.

> **Everything is based on a promise.**

Every dream you can imagine, every blessings that will ever come your way, is connected to the promises of God. Everything is based on a promise. Your job is based on a promise. The employer promises to pay the employee who promises to do their job in order to get paid. Your marriage is based on a promise. The vows each of you made to each other were a promise before God such as, richer and for poorer, sickness and in health until death do you part. Whether you are born again or unsaved, promises will occur. Many will promise you the world, but will not even give you your community. Your boss will promise you job security today, but lay you off tomorrow. Your spouse will promise you before God that he/she would never leave, but will catch a train, the first sign of trouble. God is the only one that will not renege on a promise. We will disappoint God, He will never disappoint us. God's nature will not allow Him to lie. If God said it, it must come to pass. The promise may not happen when you desire it, but God is faithful. We cannot rush God. God knows the proper timetable for your blessings to come. He knows the right season for your breakthrough. When God gives you a spiritual steak, it is always well-done. He never gives you meat that is not properly prepared. God allows it to slowly cook. God enjoys marinating our blessings. God's aim is to get impurities out of your meal. God takes His time preparing it for you. **Isaiah 55:8-9** says, *"For my thoughts are not your thoughts, neither are your ways my ways, saith the LORD. For as the heavens are higher than the earth, so are my ways higher than your ways, and my thoughts than your thoughts."* When God makes a promise, He is faithful and just to keep His end of the bargain. God's Word is His bond! I am bursting with anticipation of the blessings from the promises of God! A.W. Tozer, author of "The Knowledge of the Holy" says, "Upon God's faithfulness rests our whole hope of future blessedness. Only as He is faithful will His covenants stand and His promises be honored. Only

> **God enjoys marinating our blessings.**

as we have complete assurance that He is faithful may we live in peace and look forward with assurance to the life to come."

Oftentimes, we are rushing God to finish up our blessings. Some of us are not prepared to handle blessings from God. Some will leave the church as soon as God gives you your heart desire. Some will quit praising and worshipping God. Some will quit the choir, usher board, and greeter's ministry once they have been blessed by God. We are oftentimes too impatient to hold onto the promise of God. God knows what's best for you. The blessings that God has for you are for you. I cannot take your blessings, but you can lose your blessings when receiving them too quickly. A miscarriage occurs when a woman loses the child before the maturity date. The biggest handicap in the church is not our faith, it is our impatience. Some of us walk in tremendous faith. We literally take God at His Word, but only for 24 hours. After 24 hours of not receiving what you desired from God, we lose hope. Patience is a virtue. Virtue means God's merit on your life. II Peter 1:5-8 says, *"And beside this, giving all diligence, add to your faith virtue; and to virtue knowledge; And to knowledge temperance; and to temperance patience; and to patience godliness; And to godliness brotherly kindness; and to brotherly kindness charity. For if these things be in you, and abound, they make you that ye shall nei-*

> **The biggest handicap in the church is not our faith, it is our impatience.**

ther be barren nor unfruitful in the knowledge of our Lord Jesus Christ." Being patient while you pursue your promise is essential to your basket of fruit overflowing. Your patience with God is the key to your success. Don't rush God. When your season comes, everyone will know. God loves showcasing our blessings before our enemies.

I remember in 1979 graduating from Glen Oaks High School in Baton Rouge, Louisiana preparing to go to Paris Junior College, in Paris, Texas on a basketball scholarship. I was a McDonald's High School Basketball All-American. One morning I was preparing to get out of bed for classes and realized I was unable to move. My knees and ankles were swollen. They were as large as softballs. I had no previous injury. I had no illness that I was aware of. My roommates picked me up and drove me to the local hospital. I remember being there all day. We stayed there 8 hours awaiting the results from all the different tests. The doctor finally approached me and said my basketball career was over. The doctor said, "I was diagnosed with arthritis and I would never be able to play basketball on that level again." I spent one year on crutches. I lost so much weight during this depressed period of my life. I went from being a well built athlete, to a frail individual who was quickly losing his strength and his identity. I struggled getting in and out of bed. I used to hate to go to the bathroom at night because I would be in so much pain; I had to crawl to the bathroom. God knows how to humble you. God was starting a humbling process I was made to go through. I grew up in church, but had forgotten God. My grandfather was a pastor of a small church in Zachary, Louisiana. I went from being a high school basketball All-American to the manager of the basketball team in order to maintain my scholarship. I aspired to one day play basketball in the NBA. I went from being served to now washing the athletes clothing. God has a way of humbling you. God was drawing me back closer to Him. I realized more than ever during this time of depression, I needed the Lord much more than He needed me. I asked God to heal me of the arthritics that was causing havoc to my body. I wanted desperately to play basketball in college again. I believed God to do a supernatural healing on my body. I asked God to heal me before the next semester of school. Weeks had passed, but no sign of God. I truly in my heart believed God was going to heal me. A few weeks later, school started and I felt God let me down. I was not healed. I became angry with God. I did not want to pray or talk to anyone about church. I was a 19 year old boy away from home and had no place to turn. One night lying in my room crying, God clearly spoke to me. "Gary, you will dribble again! You will play basketball again. As a matter of fact, you will be a star. You will lead the parade." I rejoiced! I praised the Lord! But I suddenly realized, God was not talking about dribbling a basketball. He was talking about

God enlisted me to play the game of life.

dribbling for Him. God enlisted me to play the game of life. I was to be a star in God's army. Again, my promise is connected to my obedience. Oh by the way, God never did fully heal my body. I still ache from time to time. I have some good and bad days. He gave me the strength to endure hardship. I believe it keeps me humble and builds up my character for a greater assignment. I am just holding on to the promises of God. I viewed the aches and pains in my life as a storm passing over. I knew God had a greater plan for my life. Tony D. Cobbins, author of "Spiritual Storm Chasers" says, "My whole attitude about the storm changed the moment that I took the time to take in the beauty of the aftermath of the storm. It gave me a greater sense of the awesomeness of God. Only God could create such beauty in the aftermath of such chaos." I understand better now why God allowed me to experience the pain. I know now God was building my character for a greater work for Him.

There is no better character throughout the entire bible that waited on the promises of God than Abraham. Abraham was incredible. God made a promise to Abraham at the age of 75 that he would be a father of many nations. God told Abraham he would not be able to count the children. They would be like the stars in the sky. **Genesis 15:5** says, *"And he brought him forth abroad, and said, Look now toward heaven, and tell the stars, if thou be able to number them: and he said unto him, So shall thy seed be."* God told Abraham even his seed will prosper. There was one major problem; Abraham did not have any kids. The most incredible thing is not that Abraham was going to have a child, but that he believed God at 100 years old his generation would start. **Genesis 15:6** says, *"And he believed in the LORD; and he counted it to him for righteousness."* He believed that his wife, Sarah could still conceive at an old age. God called Abraham righteous because he believed. For 25 years of waiting on the promises of God, Abraham never wavered. He never doubted God no matter how old he and his wife were. He literally took God at His Word. **Romans 4:20-21** says, *"He staggered not at the promise of God through unbelief; but was strong in faith, giving glory to God; And being fully persuaded that, what he had promised, he was able also to perform."* Abraham's soul was full of confidence that the Word of God bound him to fulfill what God had promised.

Most of us would have crumbled in the first 25 days. We lack confidence in God. We lack patience with God. If God said it, it shall come to pass. God has your blessings on a spiritual layaway plan. It is yours, but He is waiting for the right time to release them into your hands. Your job is to praise, glorify, and remain faithful while you wait. Your righteousness is directly connected to your faithfulness.

Abraham waited 25 years. God wants us to wait until He feels we are ready to handle the next level blessings. We want God to respond tomorrow. Oral Roberts had a cutting edge ministry in the 70's and 80's. He was a leader in television as well as telemarketing. He set a high standard for other television ministries to follow. Ministries around the world are just starting to catch up to what Oral Roberts was doing more than 20 years ago. I enjoyed watching their television broadcast, but my true joy was in their theme song, "Something good is going to happen to you this very day." That song would motivate me to believe with God anything was possible. More importantly, that song strengthens me to give hope that the promises of God are right around the corner. I truly believed the world was at my feet, but the song messed me up. It has messed many people up. They were expecting God to show up at any moment and did not have the patience to hold on to the promises of God. Remember, your blessings are already passed out in the heavenly; you must find a way to pull them down in the flesh. Rome was not built in a day, but it was built. Your blessings will not come over night, but if you can hang in there when the water get rough, great things are coming your direction. Holding on to the promises of God will be more than a dream, it will become a reality.

CHAPTER 4
FOR DISCUSSION

1. Why is it important to hold on to the promises of God?

2. What happens every time I say, "There is a Word!"?

3. What do I mean by "God's nature will not allow Him to lie"?

4. Are we in position to rush God for our promise?

5. What is the biggest handicap in the church?

6. What happens to us when we become too impatient with God?

7. How many years did Abraham wait on the promises of God?

5

FORMED TO BE FEARLESS

In many ways, a bully is a coward. A bully oftentimes picks on people who will not fight back. He finds people who are smaller and extremely timid. A bully can spot a small frail person a mile away. His eyes are trained to spot people who are weak and unsure of themselves. He corners and intimidates you while stealing your possessions. He causes you to lose focus, self-control, and self-esteem. Ultimately, a bully's job is to cause you to walk in fear. If he gets you to walk in fear, he knows you are destroyed and useless. A bully's bark is oftentimes bigger than his bite.

Ultimately, a bully's job is to cause you to walk in fear.

Satan demonstrates these exact attributes. He

picks on the weaker vessel that has no identity of who they are. He tries to corner and intimidate while stealing your possessions such as your family, finances, homes, cars, and even your peace of mind. He's become a master of stealing, killing, and destroying anyone who refuse to stand in Christ. He is a spiritual wrecking crew all by himself. Satan tries to make you believe God doesn't love you. He causes you to believe your prayers are not being answered. Most importantly, he prides himself on causing you to be fearful. Satan gets great joy when you lack the faith to pursue your destiny. Satan also has a much bigger bark than his bite.

> **Satan gets great joy when you lack the faith to pursue your destiny.**

The age old question, how can we defeat the devil? Listen closely. Everything you need to counteract the devil's tactics, you already possess. The sleeping giant within you must be awakened. The sleeping giant within have been lying in dormant waiting on you to disturb it. **II Timothy 1:6** says it best, *"Wherefore I put thee in remembrance that thou stir up the gift of God, which is in thee by the putting on of my hands."* There must be a stirring up of the gift that God has given you. Be faithful even in afflictions according to the power of God in you. The gift is referred to fire, which, if not frequently stirred up and more fuel added, will go out. I am convinced 95 percent of the Body of Christ's problems are due to a lack of gift stirring. Paul says in **I Timothy 4:14**, *"Neglect not the gift that is in thee, which was given thee by prophecy, with the laying on of the hands of the presbytery."* This refers to the grace of God given unto us and enabling the believer to do the works of God.

> **A fearless soldier walks with a swagger.**

If our gifts are not properly used or replenished with continued grace and power from the Holy Spirit's anointing they will become powerless and useless and thus fail in their purpose. This is why men need a constant supply of the Holy Spirit. Jesus was a perfect example of living in prayer and receiving constant supply of the Holy Spirit in Luke 3:21. God created and formed us to be fearless! There's a certain air about yourself when you are fearless for God. A fearless soldier walks with a swagger. He believes God is Lord of his life through his daily dependence of faith in God. Satan has no power over us unless we allow it. A believer does not walk in fear; he walks in power, love, and a sound mind. **II Timothy 1:7** says, *"For God hath not given us the spirit of fear; but of power, and of love, and of a sound mind."* Paul was encouraging Timothy to be bold. When we allow people to intimidate us, we neutralize our effectiveness for God. The power of the Holy Spirit can help us overcome our fear of what some might say or do to us so we can continue to do God's work. A Spirit of power, love, and a sound mind is the three most important characteristics of an effective Christian fighting to reach their destiny. We are formed to be fearless!

Jeremiah was having an identity problem serving God. He told God that he could not speak and he was just a child. God reminded him in Jeremiah 1:5, *"Before I formed thee in the belly I knew thee; and before thou camest forth out of the womb I sanctified thee, and I ordained thee a prophet unto the nations."* God knew what Jeremiah would become before it happened. God knew Jeremiah and set him apart and commissioned him to do business for God before he was even born. God told Jeremiah to be not afraid of the people. He reminded Jeremiah He was with him every step of the way. Jeremiah was formed to be fearless! God is speaking the same words to us. He approved us to be awesome! He ordained us to walk in our lane traveling toward our destiny. God gave us the power to conquer kingdoms. It is impossible to walk in victory while living in fear. You can not be afraid to walk in the lane that's been ordained for you to travel.

One of my greatest fears was leaving my job as a Financial Analyst at Delta Air Lines in Atlanta, Georgia to go full-time in the ministry in January 1998. My family and I founded Voices of Faith Ministries in August 1994 with only ten people. I was working as a bi-vocational pastor, maintaining a full-time job as well as being a full-time pastor. Deep down inside, I knew working in Corporate America was not my destiny. I knew God had a greater calling for my life, but fear was keeping me from moving closer into my destiny. I knew if I was going to prosper from the things of God, a leap of faith became my only option. I was afraid, but not fearful. I took the leap of faith and gave my two-week resignation to do full-time ministry for God. In the meantime, God was testing me. Three developments were brewing doing this two-week notice causing me to weigh my options. **First**, my boss at Delta Air Lines offered me to work from home 20 hours a week to maintain my benefits with the company. He did not want me to lose the health and dental benefits with a family of six. I would only have to come in the office once a week. I could continue to use my computer from home to complete my job assignments. **Secondly**, several ministers and deacons at the church threaten to leave if I went full-time. They believed paying me a full-time salary would deplete the funds used to purchase or build a church edifice. **Thirdly**, God commissioned me for the job of full-time ministry. God said to me, "It does not matter who leaves the church, I alone am the majority." The **first** option was enticing, being able to work from home while maintaining full benefits would have lured many people, but I knew if I was going to reach my destiny, trusting God totally was the only option. The **second** option was shocking and hurting. I started thinking about the number of years we had worked so hard to build the church up only to have someone destroy it overnight. The Holy Spirit immediately gave me a scripture to deal with my pain and agony. **Isaiah 54:17** says, *"No weapon that is formed against thee shall prosper; and every tongue that shall rise* *against thee in judgment thou shalt condemn."* God gave me such a peace and serenity reminding me the same people who helped build the ministry, would not be the same who takes it to the next level. I washed my hands to prepare for the new sheep that were arriving. I no longer looked back on my yesterday. **Luke 9:62** says, *"And Jesus said unto him, No man having put his hand to the plow, and looking back, is fit for the kingdom of God."* My blessings and the fruit of my labor was in my tomorrow. The *third* option was my only option. There is no higher power to submit to but God. God was testing me, but I knew my blessings were in my obedience. I took the leap of faith and haven't looked back. January 12, 1998 will be a date I will always remember. It was the day I conquered my fears. It was the day I recognized I was formed to be fearless! Five years later, God continues to prove Himself to me to be faithful and just. We must attack our issues and problems head on. We must develop strategies for accomplishing God's task that He assigned us. Tim Hansel, in his book, "Eating Problems For Breakfast" reports, "Few people have a strategy for solving problems. In twenty years of teaching, I have found only a handful of students, and even teachers, who have a clear, concise method for approaching problems. When problems arise at inconvenient times, most of us react rather than respond. Many times, the solutions we react

> **There is no higher power to submit to but God.**

with work, at least temporarily. So, most of us don't take the time to find better, longer-lasting solutions."

Do you realize fear will cause you to run outside of your lane God assigned for your life? All of your blessings and breakthroughs in life will come to you while running in your lane. You must run the race that God has set forth for you to run. Your lane is unique and special. Your lane is anointed. It is commissioned and ordained for you to prosper. Your lane has your DNA only. I am a big fan of track and field. I love to watch the sprint relays and the 100 and 200 meters. I am constantly amazed at the number of track runners and their team who are disqualified for running outside of their lane. They oftentimes get themselves in trouble looking in their opponent's lane to check out the competition. Whenever you take your eyes off your lane, it causes you to stumble. The devil's job is to push you outside of your lane because he knows you lack the anointing and fighting power in someone else' lane. If you can remain in your lane through the good and the difficult days in your life, blessings and prosperity is immediately on the way. God formed you to be fearless so that no obstacle placed in your lane will cause you to make a detour. You have been ordained to cross the finish line in the lane you were assigned.

Your lane has your DNA only.

Football is a game for warriors. It is not designed for the weak and fainthearted. Football is a mental as well as physical game. A football player is trained to be fearless. He is equipped to go the distance. Throughout the course of a game, it never ceased to amaze me that the players who are often hurt are the ones who go half speed during the game. They are often worried about their opponent and not the assignment they've been given to perform their job. They play as if they are expected to get hurt. They play with a timid spirit. Satan's job is to get you to walk around through life half speed. He gets great joy seeing you blindsided and carried out on a stretcher. He wants you to constantly look over your shoulder for your enemy. Satan's assignment is to make you timid and afraid of life itself. Your job is to develop a warrior's mentality. Your mission is to enter the playing field with a fearless attitude and to cause your opponent to tremble. God formed you to be fearless! Now is the time to strap on the helmet, put on the shoulder pads, and let the enemy know he is in a fight for his life and you will score the winning touchdown.

Jeremiah did not allow his fear, anger, and disappointment to overtake him. He did not allow the whispers and the plots from the people against his life to deter him from doing the will of God. Jeremiah was frustrated because he assumed God did not care. He felt God had deceived him concerning ministry. He even vowed not to mention God's name to anyone, but there was a fire trapped inside that would not allow him to stop ministering. **Jeremiah 20:9** says, *"Then I said, I will not make* *mention of him, nor speak any more in his name. But his word was in mine heart as a burning fire shut up in my bones, and I was weary with forbearing, and I could not stay."* Jeremiah was determined to quit speaking the word of the Lord; but it became as a fire shut up in his bones and he was weary of holding it back. He knew his survival was in his fearlessness. The fire within continued the flames burning when he became frustrated. Notice, the fire within kept Jeremiah on course to fight for his destiny. The fire kept his gifts stirred which allowed his fearlessness to wreck havoc on the devil.

Does the devil have you on his "Do not mess with" list?

Romans 8:15-16 says, *"For you have not received the spirit of bondage again to fear; but ye have received the Spirit of adoption, whereby we cry, Abba, Father. The Spirit itself beareth witness with our spirit, that we are the children of God."* God did not give us the spirit and nature of Satan. You have not received a spirit of slavery to relapse again into fear and terror. God gave us the Spirit of freedom and "sonship" to break every bondage and stronghold. As sons and daughters to God, we share the same rights and privileges as one born in the family. Slaves were never allowed to say, "Abba, Father." You have been given the authority to be fearless. We are no longer fearful slaves. We now are the Master's children. We have the right to eat from the same vineyard as Abraham, Moses, Elijah, and Paul.

Does the devil have you on his "Do not mess with" list? Does Satan know your name? Have you entered the game? Have your name been called? Does he even have your telephone number? There's a list of people Satan has listed on a roster that he has given to his cohorts to not mess with. Satan knows who has the power of the Holy Spirit deep down inside of them. He wants no dealings with them. Satan has been bruised and beat up by these warriors. Satan was afraid of Paul. God allowed Paul to perform some incredible miracles. Paul's handkerchiefs alone brought much healing as soon as the sick touched it. In Acts 19, there were vagabond Jews who had witness the extraordinary miracles of Paul. A vagabond Jew was a roving Jew traveling from place to place practicing witchcraft. They witnessed Paul healing the sick using Jesus' name. The vagabond Jews called some men together who had evil spirits and tried to cast them out using Jesus' name. The demons did not have these vagabond Jews on their "do not mess with" list. They said in **Acts 19:15**, *"And the evil spirit answered and said, Jesus I know, and Paul I know; but who are ye?"* The demon leaped upon the vagabond Jews and began to beat them leaving them naked and wounded. The devil knows who are fearless and who are playing church? Does he have your number? Jesus would cause fear and trembling with the demons. They hated to see Him coming. **Matthew 8:28-29** says, *"And when he was come to the other side into the country of the Gergesenes,* *there met him two possessed with devils, coming out of the tombs, exceeding fierce, so that no man might pass by that way. And, behold, they cried out, saying, What have we to do with thee, Jesus, thou Son of God? art thou come hither to torment us before the time?"* We must walk in the same Spirit and boldness to wreck havoc upon the devil and his cohorts.

Luke 10 tells us of Jesus anointing some disciples to go into the cities winning lost souls for the kingdom. He sent them on a business trip. Their assignment was to do business for God. Jesus anoints each one and gives them the power to minister to the lost. Upon there return, they bragged to Jesus about them casting out demons using His name, but not about who were saved. Jesus says in **Luke 10:18-19**, *"And he said unto them, I beheld Satan as lightning fall from heaven. Behold, I give unto you power to tread on serpents and scorpions, and over all the power of the enemy: and nothing shall by any means hurt you."* Jesus was not impressed that they cast out demons. They were formed to be fearless. He wanted to know who received salvation. In **Luke 10:20**, Jesus adds, *"Notwithstanding in this rejoice not, that the spirits are subject unto you; but rather rejoice, because your names are written in heaven."* Power over demons should not be the source of joy, but sonship evidenced by one's name being written in heaven.

CHAPTER 5
FOR DISCUSSION

1. Why are we formed to be fearless?

2. What happens to a bully if we fight back?

3. How can the devil be defeated?

4. What were the three developments that occurred doing my two-week notice to cause me to weigh my options?

5. What happens if you run out of your assigned lane?

6. Does the anointing assist you in defeating the devil?

7. Does the devil have you on his "Do not mess with" list?

6

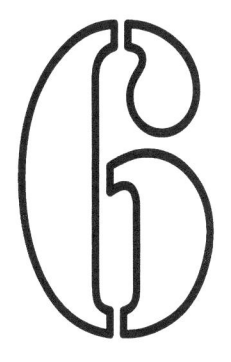

FAILURE IS NOT YOUR FINAL DESTINATION

Our society has spoon fed us to be successful. We have been told to get an education to help further advance our careers and to move up the corporate ladder. Society tells us how to dress for success. Our society has even taught us how to walk upright and speak the correct language to fit in. We are told how to pursue greatness. We are taught how to get out of debt. Our society teaches us how to invest money wisely. Marriage counselors teach an unhappy couple how to love again. Preachers and priest teach disciples how to live a holy and righteous life. They give the secrets on how to make it into the kingdom of heaven. Lawyers show us how to fight to win court cases. Doctors demonstrate to us the proper way to perform surgery. Police officers show us how to correctly enforce the law. The President of the United States even shows us how to effectively run our country. When it comes to success, our society is loaded with ammunition and antidotes.

Sadly, no one has prepared us for failure. No one has shared with us the secrets of failure. No one teaches how to handle a job layoff. There are no instructors to share with us on how to be an outcast in society. We have no narrators teaching us the dramas of life. Failure in our society is a taboo. Just the mention of the word failure, causes the average person to frown. We teach our children that failure is not in our dictionary. When we see failure traveling down the street, we make a u-turn to avoid an accident. No one likes failure or is interested in getting to know him. We have not been trained how to fail, but how to succeed. Failure happens much more often than success.

> **God uses failure to test your patience and endurance.**

I have great news; Failure is not your final destination! Failure is just a bump on the road leading to success. Failure is stepping stones God uses as the pieces to build the bridge to get you to your destination. God uses failure to build your character. Failure does not mean no with God, it just means that He has you on a delayed system. God uses failure to test your patience and endurance. God discovers a lot about us doing our disappointments.

Samson did not allow his failure with Delilah to

be his final destination. Samson was a nazarite man. A nazarite was a person who vowed to be set apart for God's service. In this case, Samson's parents made the vow for him. A nazarite could not cut his hair, touch a dead body, or drink anything containing alcohol. Samson was seduced by a philistine woman named Delilah who lived in the valley of Sorek. Samson was in love with Delilah. **Judges 16:5** says, *"And the lords of the Philistines came up unto her, and said unto her, Entice him, and see wherein his great strength lieth, and by what means we may prevail against him, that we may bind him to afflict him: and we will give thee every one of us eleven hundred pieces of silver."* Samson shared with Delilah that his incredible strength was in the long locks of his hair. Delilah betrayed the secret of his strength to the Philistines, who captured him, cut his hair, and led him away in chains to a city called Gaza. Samson became weak like any other man. Because of Samson's disobedience, the Spirit of God departed from him. Samson's relationship with God had deteriorated so much that he didn't even realize God had left him. He took his strength as well as God's presence for granted. God offered Samson all he would ever need, yet Samson chose instead to put himself into Delilah's deceitful hands. Samson was determined not to allow his failure with Delilah to be his final destination. **Judges 16:26** says, *"And Samson said unto the lad that held him by the hand, Suffer me that I may feel the pillars whereupon the house* *standeth, that I may lean upon them."* Samson asked God to correct his mistake by avenging his adversaries. He wanted to die in battle and be remembered for victory, not failure. **Judges 16:30** says, *"And Samson said, Let me die with the Philistines. And he bowed himself with all his might; and the house fell upon the lords, and upon all the people that were therein."* God still loved Samson. God was willing to hear Samson's prayer of confession and repentance and use him this final time. Don't let guilty feelings over sin prevent you from God. He is the only means of restoration. No matter how long you have been away from God, He is always ready to restore you to your rightful place with Him. Remember, failure is not your final destination; it is a bump in the road toward success.

Moses was another character in the bible that failed, but did not allow his mistakes to be final. God told Moses to speak to the rock to bring forth water; Moses out of anger towards the complaining and bickering Israelites struck the rock twice. **Numbers 20:11-12** says, *"And Moses lifted up his hand, and with his rod he smote the rock twice: and the water came out abundantly, and the congregation drank, and their beasts also. And the LORD spake unto Moses and Aaron, Because ye believed me not, to sanctify me in the eyes of the children of Israel, therefore ye shall not bring this congregation into the land which I have given them."* Moses disobedience prevented him from entering the Promise Land flowing with milk and honey. Was God's punishment of Moses too harsh? After all, the Israelites nagged him, slandered his name, and even rebelled against both him and God. Moses was a leader who represented God. He was God's human spokesman. Because of this great responsibility to the people, he could not be let off lightly. By striking the rock, Moses disobeyed God's direct command and dishonored God in the presence of His people. Moses was determined not to have failure be his final destination. Moses begged God seeking permission to go over to the Promised Land. **Deuteronomy 3:25-26** says, *"I pray thee, let me go over, and see the good land that is beyond Jordan, that goodly mountain, and Lebanon. But the LORD was wroth with me for your sakes, and would not hear me: and the LORD said unto me, Let it suffice thee; speak no more unto me of this matter."* God had made it clear that Moses would not enter the Promised Land. God even told Moses not to bring up the request to Him again. In the book of Numbers, God instructed Moses to get to Mount Abarim to see the Promised Land and prepare to die. Watch closely to what Moses did. He did not want to be remembered as a failure. **Numbers 27:16-17** says, *"Let the LORD, the God of the spirits of all flesh, set a man over the congregation. Which may go out before them, and which may go in before them, and which may lead them out, and which may bring them in; that the congregation of the LORD be not as sheep which have no shepherd."* Moses did not want to leave his work without making sure a new leader was ready to replace him. Moses spoke to God concerning Israel's great need. He compared it to a shepherd and his sheep. He prayed for a leader who, like a shepherd going before the sheep and leading them in and out to pasture, would care for Israel. First, he asked God to help him find a replacement. Secondly, when God selected Joshua to replace Moses, he trained Joshua in a variety of tasks to ease the transition into Joshua's new position. Moses told the Israelites that Joshua had the authority and the ability to lead the nation into the Promised Land. Moses did not want God and the people to remember him as a failure. Failure was not Moses final destination. God loved Moses. God is sovereign choosing to do what He wants to do. Even though Moses was preparing to die, he was still seeking to please God. God rewarded Moses by allowing him to see the Promised Land. **Deuteronomy 34:4-5** says, *"And the LORD said unto him, This is the land which I sware unto Abraham, unto Isaac, and unto Jacob, saying, I will give it unto thy seed: I have caused thee to see it with thine eyes, but thou shalt not go over thither. So Moses the servant of the LORD died there in the land of Moab, according to the word of the LORD."* Notice, after Moses' failure, he was remembered in Deuteronomy 34:5 as "The servant of the Lord." Moses was called servant of the Lord 18 times throughout the bible. Moses failure did not become his final destination. We also know Moses and Elijah appeared with a transfigured Jesus and on a high mountain in Matthew 17.

The average entrepreneur fails at least four times before success knocks at his door. Many entrepreneurs have filed bankruptcy and gone on to become millionaires. Entrepreneurs have succeeded because they refused to take no for an answer. Their drive, determination, and dedication have been the needed tools to succeed.

Five years ago, God directed me to look for land to build our new church. I visited every vacant lot and property within a 10 mile radius. Any property that had a for sale sign, I pursued. I was turned down at least 100 times. I knew every owner on a first name basis. I was determined not to fail God. I knew the destiny God had for my life and I desperately wanted to pursue it. I was looking for land that had for sale signs listed on the property. God spoke in my spirit, "Your land does not have a for sale sign on the property." Months of searching for land were beginning to drain me. Finally, God revealed our property to me in Stone Mountain, Georgia. A property I must had passed a thousand times. There was no for sale sign posted. I went on the land and began to worship God for His faithfulness. I went to the Gwinnett County office to find the owner. He lived in Sarasota, Florida. He agreed to sell 20 acres of land to us for $300,000. I was determined not to have failure as my final destination.

> **Failure is not permanent; it's a stepping stone for greatness.**

Failure is not permanent; it's a stepping stone for greatness. Jesus told Peter that he would fail. Satan was going to cause him to stumble. **Luke 22:31-32** says, *"And the Lord said, Simon, Simon, behold, Satan hath desired to have you, that he may sift you as wheat. But I have prayed for thee, that thy faith fail not: and when thou art converted, strengthen thy brethren."* Notice this important fact; Jesus never stops Satan from causing Peter to fail. He prays for Peter that his faith fails him not. Remember, failure builds character. God was developing Peter's character.

King Saul was afraid to lead God's people. **I Samuel 10:22** says, *"Therefore they inquired of the LORD further, if the man should yet come thither. And the LORD answered, Behold, he hath hid himself among the stuff."* When the Israelites assembled to choose a king, Saul knew he was the chosen one. Instead of coming forth, he hid among military baggage. We are often like King Saul. We hide from responsibilities because we are afraid of failure. Trust God's provision rather than your feelings of adequacy. If God gave you the vision, He will provide the provision.

Paul was a prime example on how to handle failure and disappointments. Paul was a man who could heal the sick, cast out demons, yet could not heal himself. Three times Paul asked God to remove the thorn, each time God refused. God was using Paul's pain as character building. **II Corinthians 12:8** says, *"For this thing I besought the Lord* *thrice, that it might depart from me."* This thorn was a hindrance to Paul's ministry. He prayed to God for its removal; but God refused. Paul's attitude blessed me. Failure was not going to be his final destination with God. **II Corinthians 12:9-10** says, *"And he said unto me, My grace is sufficient for thee: for my strength is made perfect in weakness. Most gladly therefore will I rather glory in my infirmities, that the power of Christ may rest upon me. Therefore I take pleasure in infirmities, in reproaches, in necessities, in persecutions, in distresses for Christ's sake: for when I am weak, then am I strong."* Although God did not remove Paul's thorn, He promised to demonstrate His power in Paul. Paul learned to glorify God in his infirmities so that the power of Christ could rest upon him. Failure was not Paul's final destination. We must experience some pain in life to succeed. Larry Richards, author of "When Life Is Unfair" says, "I can't tell you that what lies in your future will only hurt a little bit. But I can tell you that, because God is both Almighty and truly Good, He will see to it that through your suffering good will come. Whatever the future holds, God will be there for you. He will stay with you. And God will use the unfair things in your life for good."

God takes us through a process. There are different stages we go through to experience success. We must be willing to suffer and be ridiculed in the beginning to eat from the harvest later. A writer once gave five stages to reaching your destiny. **First**

stage: *"Afraid of being a fool."* This stage is critical to the beginning of your success. This individual is afraid to trust God and take the leap of faith. They are afraid of what others might say if they launch out into the deep and fail. I ran from God many years before accepting my calling into the ministry. I truly was afraid of what others would think about me. I also thought I was not qualified for the calling of preaching the Gospel of Jesus Christ. **Second stage:** *"Looking like a fool."* This stage is extremely important to maintain your composure as well as your pride. This stage will make you quit believing in your dream. They laugh at you in this stage. They mock you in this stage. You are the center piece around the water cooler at work. When we first launched our ministry in August 1994, we had about ten members. There was this one individual who would laugh and make fun of me about our church. He would say things like, "Pastor Hawkins, I know it was a traffic jam getting out of the church parking lot on last Sunday?" He would say other things such as, "Did you break your record of two visitors in attendance yet?" He was truly a comedian. I must admit, I used to laugh at him myself. When you know what God has called you to do, you can laugh with others while pursuing your destiny. **Third stage:** *"You become a fool."* This stage may be the most crucial stage of them all. This is the twilight stage. A twilight stage is when everything is dark in your life. You don't know which way to turn. You have no directions. You don't know east from west nor south from north. This stage causes you to feel totally confused and worthless. You feel like you are on the blink of self-destruction. You feel like quitting. In this stage, you feel all hope has been zapped away. **Fourth stage:** *"Successful entrepreneurship."* This stage confirms your self-worth. This stage says that you have arrived. This stage affirms that God ordained you for the assignment. You are the new kid on the block in this stage. In this stage, God allows you to reach your destiny. He allows you to pick from the Promised Land. God reveals to you that the land truly is flowing with milk and honey. **Fifth Stage:** *"Genius."* In this stage, you have conquered the Promised Land. You are no longer the new kid on the block, you now own the block. In this stage, people come to you for advice on how to grow their business. In this stage, buildings are erected in your name. Freeways and bridges are dedicated to you for community services. You become known as a Philanthropist, one who devotes time, energy, and money to his fellowman. In this stage, you begin to write books and speak at growth seminars sharing with others your success story.

CHAPTER 6
FOR DISCUSSION

1. Has anyone prepared you for failure?

2. Is failure your final destination with God?

3. Did Samson allow his mistake with Delilah to be his final destination?

4. What did Moses do that prevented him from entering the Promised Land?

5. How many times does an entrepreneur fail before he succeeds?

6. Was Jesus building up Peter's character by allowing Satan to sift him as wheat?

7. What are the five stages we must experience in reaching our destiny?

7

DISCOVERING OUR CIRCLE OF STRENGTH

Sometimes life can be overwhelming. The issues of life can be so terrifying and frightening that it can become extremely difficult to keep our heads above water. Oftentimes our minds are so clouded, we don't know if we are coming or going. We have a difficult time discerning morning from nightfall. The issues of life have a way of stopping you right in your track. Our issues can become so unbearable that we lose focus on our destiny. Losing a loved one can play a tremendous role on ones life. The lost of a job can even cause great depression. Discovering a spouse's unfaithfulness can be devastating. Even feeling rejected by a friend, co-worker, and during a job interview can leave scars for a lifetime. How do we handle life's pitfalls? We must discover our circle of strength to prevent the issues of life from stopping us from reaching our destiny. Discovering your circle of strength will help you get out of the rut you are struggling with.

I know who I am in the Lord. I have gone through tough times and suffering, but I know without a shadow of a doubt my place in the kingdom of God. I did not discover who I was during good times in my life. I did not recognize my strength while saying my vows at the wedding ceremony. I did not understand my net worth while studying for my MBA in Financial Management at National University in San Diego, California. It's not when you enlist in the military when you discover your strengths, strong points, characteristics, and attributes. Your circle of strength is not discovered when you join the church on a Sunday morning or a Wednesday night. I discovered who I was when the bottom fell out of my life. I discovered who I was when I had no where else to turn but Jesus Christ. It was during the most difficult time of God testing me when I discovered my strength. My strength was not in material or wealth. My circle of strength was in knowing Jesus Christ loves me and has a plan for my life.

King David discovered his circle of strength the hard way. God had to allow him to go through some suffering to get his attention. King David was in awe of the beauty of Bath-sheba. **II Samuel 11:2** says, *"And it came to pass in an eveningtide, that*

David arose from off his bed, and walked upon the roof of the king's house: and from the roof he saw a woman washing herself; and the woman was very beautiful to look upon." King David wanted Bath-sheba desperately, but there was one major problem. Bath-sheba was married. Her husband, Uriah was off fighting a war on King David's behalf. King David slept with Bath-sheba and she became pregnant. Isn't it interesting, King David could have had any woman of his choice, but he chooses a woman who was already married? We oftentimes make decisions similar to King David. We are given choices from God that will totally bless us, but we choose the ones that oftentimes bring curses on us as well as our family. King David sends for her husband, Uriah to come home to spend quality time with his wife, but Uriah refuses. This act would let Bath-sheba know that he was the one who had sent for her husband and that he was sending him home for the purpose of concealing their sin together, but the plan failed. King David asked Uriah why he would not go and visit his wife whom he has not seen in weeks or even months? Uriah gives King David a powerful response. **II Samuel 11:11** says, *"And Uriah said unto David, The ark, and Israel, and Judah, abide in tents; and my lord Joab, and the servants of my lord, are encamped in the open fields; shall I then go into mine house, to eat and to drink, and to lie with my wife? as thou livest, and as thy soul liveth, I will not do this thing."* King David really could not conceive such a thing—a man refusing to go to his wife and home when he had the opportunity. Uriah had more integrity than King David. King David's next step was to get Uriah killed. King David wrote a letter to Joab who was Uriah's commander. King David sent the letter by the hands of Uriah. The letter contained information about Uriah. He was holding a letter that contained his own death sentence. Uriah was killed in the war. King David tried to cover up sin by creating more sin. King David is about to discover his circle of strength.

A child is born unto King David and Bath-sheba. The child was born healthy, but God struck the child with sickness due to King David's sin. King David immediately began to fast and lay all night before the Lord beseeching and pleading with God to allow the child to live. King David fasted for 7 days. We oftentimes discover our circle of strength during the difficult periods in our lives. King David was in a very uncomfortable feeling. He had no control of the situation. He was helpless and needed God. King David said to God in **Psalms 51:1-3**, *"Have mercy upon me, O God, according to thy lovingkindness: according unto the multitude of thy tender mercies blot out my transgressions. Wash me thoroughly from mine iniquity, and cleanse me from my sin. For I acknowledge my transgressions: and my sin is ever before me."* King David was pleading for his life and complete restoration with God. He even asked God to create within him a new heart and renew a right spirit within him. King

David pleaded with God not to remove His presence from him and take away the power of the Holy Spirit that rest upon him. King David understood he was anointed and chosen by God to prosper in the kingdom and he needed God's total forgiveness. He knew the child was sick and in pain because of his direct disobedience to God. It is in this environment, God allows our character to build. King David needed to totally trust God and get back to the basics of doing the things God expected out of him. King David knew he could never reach his destiny without God being on his side. He knew the devil would keep him bounded up. He desperately needed God to restore him and heal his child. God allowed the child to die.

The child was now dead, but King David's servant was afraid to tell him. King David heard their whispering and asked, "Is the child dead?" And they answered, "The child is dead." As soon as King David heard his son was dead, he immediately gets up to wash himself. **II Samuel 12:20** says, *"Then David arose from the earth, and washed, and anointed himself, and changed his apparel, and came into the house of the LORD, and worshipped: then he came to his own house; and when he required, they set bread before him, and he did eat."* King David servants were somewhat confused. They were expecting King David to continue to mourn because of his son's death. Usually the relatives mourned and wept until the third or fourth day; and friends and distant relatives came to see them, and to urge them to eat and put on other garments. **II Samuel 12:21** says, *"Then said his servants unto him, What thing is this that thou hast done? thou didst fast and weep for the child, while it was alive; but when the child was dead, thou didst rise and eat bread."* David explains to them that he fasted and wept for the child while he was alive, but fasting and weeping after his son's death will not bring the child back to him.

> **God is waiting for you to rise up from your sulking.**

King David gives us a seven step blueprint in II Samuel 12:20 on how to get restored with God. He demonstrates to us how to recapture and rediscover our circle of strength. **First,** *"David arose from the earth."* David was demonstrating to us that since the death of his son, he would no longer sit around the house and have a pity party for himself. He would no longer be miserable over things he has no control. Some of us have been in misery for so long; God is waiting for you to rise up from your sulking. **Secondly,** *"King David washed himself."* Washing yourself is so important. Washing represents a cleansing. By washing yourself, you are asking God to clean up the muck, filth and sin in your life and put on a whole new glory. You are getting rid of the old man, Adam and putting on the new man, Jesus Christ. Once you have humbled yourself and totally surrendered back to God, God is ready to restore you and use you for His glory. Our attitudes must never indicate to others and to God that the sun rises and sets upon us. We must always recognize God as Lord. **Thirdly**, *"King David anoints himself."* Why is it so important to anoint yourself? I often feel we don't anoint ourselves enough. God has made us kings and priest. He has given us the power and the authority to cast out demons and bind and loose strongholds in our lives. What does it mean by anointing yourself? We must make sure we've approved ourselves. So many people are waiting on someone else to validate them. We wait on our boss to tell us we are doing a great

> **A depression sets in because you feel your net worth is non-existence.**

job before we recognize it ourselves. We want to hear our spouse tell us that we are great husbands and wives and get angry when they don't. A depression sets in because you feel your net worth is non-existence. David gives us a glimpse of the Holy of Holies. The moment the veil split in two, we had the right to go to God ourselves for cleansing and forgiveness. We do not have to wait for the approval of others, just God. Jesus oftentimes prayed for himself. It's not selfish to pray for yourself. When your prayer and desire is to bring glory to God, He invites our prayer request. You have to get to a point in your life where you anoint yourself for the glory of God. Lay hands on yourself and declare that you are healed, anointed, and righteous in the sight of God. You do not have to wait for someone to prophesy into your life. I suggest you even tell yourself that today is going to be a great day in the Lord!

I promise you, it will be. Start expecting better results from your prayers. King David wasn't waiting on somebody around him to anoint him. There will be people in your life who likes to see you down and out. They enjoy seeing you in misery. They love to know your spouse just left you and your children are disobedient. There was a woman in San Diego who I used to work with at General Dynamics. She always gave the ladies advice on how she would not tolerate the things they were experiencing with their husbands. She told them, "I would never cut the grass at my house. I would never do a man's job when my husband is with me." Over a period of time, several women started leaving their spouses after allowing this woman to break up a happy home. A few months later, one of the women who left her spouse on this woman's advice drove to her house to visit her. When she arrived she was stunned to find the woman in the yard cutting her own grass while the husband was in the house. She was an expert at giving advice to others, but was not receiving it for herself. The bottom line is we must anoint ourselves! **Fourthly**, *"King David changed his clothes."* Changing your clothes is extremely important. In many ways, the clothes represented hurt. The clothes represent memory of a certain event in your life. I oftentimes run across old clothing in my closet that I thought I had tossed and it immediately reminded me of events I spent with a certain individual. David did not want to remember the pain and suffering he was experiencing by the clothes he was wearing. By removing the old clothes from your body, you are suggesting that it is a brand new day. People will often associate events in your life with your clothing. There are some folk that can tell what you were wearing five years ago to the day. Changing your clothes is important to moving to the next level with God. **Fifthly**, *"King David came into the house of the Lord."* Notice the first place King David visited after putting on new clothes was the house of the Lord. David made it personal. He knew he had to get back in close relationship with God. King David knew this was not the time to make his rounds visiting relatives, but to re-acquaint himself with God. Tommy Barnett, author of "Hidden Power" says, "When we don't give time to God, in His love He may force us into situations where we must spend time with Him. Some of us are afraid of being face to face, eyeball to eyeball with God. We don't know what He'll say to us. We feel that if we're with Him for too long, He might summon us to an impossible level of service or humiliate us with our sins." The house of the Lord represented a safe haven. It represented peace and serenity. Most importantly, the house of the Lord represented where God rested His glory. David knew he had to find a place in his life of solitude. David wanted to get to the house of the Lord so that he could call on the name of the Lord without interruption. **Sixth**, *"King David worshipped the Lord."* Worshipping the Lord is a powerful thing. Worshipping God is what brings Him into your presence. King David understood this concept. David knew he had messed up with God and he needed an intimate conversation with God by ushering the Lord to him by his worship. David needed a place of solitude so that he could freely worship God and not be concerned with others reaction. David was accustomed to worshipping God. When the Ark of the Lord was recovered and brought back to Israel, David shouted and danced before the Lord and the people. **II Samuel 6:14** says, *"And David danced before the LORD with all his might; and David was girded with a linen ephod."* We must at all times be in a worship mode. Worship is the key to a successful conversation with God. The **seventh** and final thing King David did to discover his circle of strength; *"King David came to his own house."* There is no place like home. Our home is our castle. Our home can sometimes cure a lot of hurt in our lives. Every now and then my wife, Debbie and I along with our children drive home to Baton Rouge, Louisiana and Beaumont, Texas to visit our family. It seems whatever is ailing us, home has a way of fixing it. Notice, the seventh thing David did represented completion. Whenever you discover your circle of strength you'll always discover wisdom along with it. The seventh day always means rest or completion. A lot of us are still operating our lives on the sixth day which is worship. We must get to a point in our lives where we turn our worship into

> **The seventh day always means rest or completion.**

rest. Rest is the assurance that God heard our prayers through our worship. Rest means we now have the authority to pursue our destiny with God. King David returns home and ate food from a week of fasting. He even conversed with his servants. Afterward, King David comforts his wife. **II Samuel 12:24** says, *"And David comforted Bathsheba his wife, and went in unto her, and lay with her: and she bare a son, and he called his name Solomon: and the LORD loved him."* God is absolutely amazing! God uses the same woman, Bath-sheba to bring glory to Him. He could have used any other woman, but instead blessed Bath-sheba to birth a son who later would become king of Israel. What that suggests is God will not only forgive us, but He will restore us to our rightful place in the kingdom of God. Bath-sheba birthed a son and his name was called Solomon. Solomon means peace. It suggests that King David was at peace with God and himself. Every time he saw Solomon, it reminded him of the peace he made with God. Solomon was given by God more wisdom than any other man on the face of the earth. God loved Solomon very much. **II Samuel 12:25** says, *"And he sent by the hand of Nathan the prophet; and he called his name Jedidiah, because of the LORD."* Jedidiah means beloved of Jehovah. King David understood that wisdom in knowing God is the only thing that would restore him.

God is looking for some people who He can give a Jedidiah experience to. God is searching for people who have discovered their circle of strength is the LORD! I am not worthy to write this book, **"Fighting For Your Destiny"** but God has given me a Jedidiah experience. I am not worthy to stand before an awesome congregation at Voices of Faith Ministries in Stone Mountain, Georgia and preach the Gospel of Jesus Christ. He has restored me into my rightful place in the kingdom of God to do business for Him until He returns. I recognize I am operating on God's grace and mercy. I am oftentimes nervous before I speak before God's people. I literally take God's assignment serious. God does not have time for games. When you discover your circle of strength; you will discover your rightful place in the kingdom of God. Remember, it is not doing the great times when you discover who you are; it is in the most complex time of your life, when God will reveal Himself to you. It is an opportunity for God to find out your character. I beseech and encourage you to hold on a little tighter during the storm. God is preparing you for greatness! God is looking for people who are starving to please Him! He is looking for anyone who has a desire to be used for the Gospel's sake. Tommy Tenney, author of "The God Chasers" says, "He is not going to pour out His Spirit where He doesn't find hunger. He looks for the hungry. Hungry means you're dissatisfied with the way it has been because it forced you to live without Him in His fullness. He only comes when you are ready to turn it all over to Him. God is coming back to repossess His Church, but you have to be hungry."

> **God does not have time for games.**

CHAPTER 7
FOR DISCUSSION

1. Why is it so important to discover your circle of strength?

2. How did King David discover his circle of strength?

3. What was Bath-sheba first husband's name?

4. What is the seven step blueprint King David used to restore his relationship back with God?

5. What did King David and Bath-sheba named their child?

6. What does "Solomon" mean?

7. What is a "Jedidiah Experience"?

8

WALKING IN VICTORY

God is desperate to bless you. If we can ever receive this in our spirit, the world will be our footstool. God want more than ever to give you your heart's desire. God is desperate to bring a blessing upon your life. God is willing to meet you where you are. If your faith is small, God will hand out nuggets to keep you encouraged. If you have so great a faith that will cause the devil to tremble, God will gladly give you the entire chicken.

I no longer ask God for things I can accomplished on my own. I am no longer seeking nuggets from God. I have gotten spoiled from the goodness of God and now desire more of Him. I ask God for things I cannot do on my own. I want the entire chicken. God does not need great faith to work a miracle; He needs willing participants for the task at hand. God is looking for mustard seed faith. **Matthew 17:20** says, *"And Jesus said unto them, Because of your unbelief: for verily I say unto you, If ye have faith as a grain of mustard seed, ye shall say unto this mountain, Remove hence to yonder place; and it shall remove; and nothing shall be impossible unto you."* God does not need a lot of faith to bless you, but faith plays a major role in receiving a blessing. It is impossible to please God without walking in faith and obedience. Faith is a prerequisite to walking in victory. God is so desperate to bless you that He is traveling to and from the earth looking for whoever will be obedient for a breakthrough. **II Chronicles 16:9** says, *"For the eyes of the LORD run to and fro throughout the whole earth, to show himself strong in the behalf of them whose heart is perfect toward him. Herein thou hast done foolishly: therefore from henceforth thou shalt have wars."* Make no mistake about it, God desire is for you to prosper and be victorious in the things of God. In order for us to walk in victory, we must be purpose driven. You will not arrive at your destiny by accident. Directions are needed to get to your destination with God. When I visit my mother in Baton Rouge, Louisiana, I don't just get on any interstate or freeway believing it will get me to her house. I need to first know what direction I am heading. When driving to my mother's house

> **God is looking for mustard seed faith.**

from Atlanta, Georgia, I take I-85 south to Montgomery, Alabama. When leaving Montgomery I take I-65 south to Mobile, Alabama. After leaving Mobile, I take I-10 west into the state of Louisiana and to the city of Baton Rouge. I already knew the directions to get to my mother's house. God is your spiritual compass able and ready to lead you into your destiny. We must be willing vessels ready to be used for God's glory.

> **The devil tries to clip your wings before take-off.**

The devil hates it when you get your directions right with God. Satan understands it is extremely difficult to stop an 18 wheeler truck at full speed. His job is to flatten your tires before the journey. The devil tries to clip your wings before take-off. He realizes if he can keep you grounded, you are no threat to him and his cohorts. We have been ordained to take over and possess the land. We must begin to look victorious! Our behavior patterns must represent a victorious lifestyle. Our speech patterns must sound like a man who has conversed with God face to face. Our actions must be that of Jacob wrestling with an angel until the break of dawn saying, "I am not going to let you go, until you bless me." We must walk upright, shoulders straight, head lifted with the assurance that victory is on the way. If your self-esteem is low and you lack the faith to make it happen. I suggest you "fake it until you make it."

Our faith must be incredible with God. I believe

we have lost out on many blessings because of our lack of faith in God. I am reminded of a story of a man who was visiting the Grand Canyon. He was touring the place from the top of a mountain. He was taking pictures with his camera of the beauty of nature and the depth of the Grand Canyon. As he was snapping a shot of the breathtaking scenery, he slipped and fell into the Grand Canyon. As he was falling, a branch withheld his fall. As he was dangling from the branch he yelled, "Is anybody out there?" God answered, "I am here!" The man said, "God, please get me down from the branch to safe ground." God said, "Do you believe I can save you? Do you believe I can get you to safe ground?" The man said, "Yes, Lord I believe!" God said, "Let go of the branch and I will catch you!" The man paused for a few seconds and yelled, "Is anyone else out there?" Our blessings are clogged up because we lack the faith in God to totally trust Him.

> **A faith walker starts to perform before the blessings come.**

We have been given the measure of faith by God to exercise it for His glory. How do we get this faith? Kenneth E. Hagin, author of "Understanding The Anointing" says, "There is a measure of the Holy Spirit in the believer for a certain purpose, but an anointing comes upon you to stand in the office (or ministry) to which God has called you. Although it's the same Holy Spirit, it's a different anointing." The moment you accept Christ as Savior, the moment

Christ enters your life, God grants you this incredible power of faith. **I John 5:4-5** says, *"For whatsoever is born of God overcometh the world: and this is the victory that overcometh the world, even our faith. Who is he that overcometh the world, but he that believeth that Jesus is the Son of God?"* God has given you the power to overcome whatever issues you are dealing with. He has given you the power to overcome issues on your job, and issues in your own household. God has given you the power to take authority over your finances, but we lack the faith in God to manifest our blessings. We don't walk like we are in authority. We don't think like we are in control of our destiny. I am a faith walker! A faith walker walks with a swagger. They walk as if God is about to open up the flood gates and pour them out a blessing where they will not have room enough to receive. A faith walker starts to perform before the blessings come. They start pre-packing bags and loading up boxes to move into their new home. A faith walker will clean his car from the inside out to prepare to sell it or trade it in on their new automobile. I tell my congregation and couples, if their desire is to have a child, start decorating a baby room in your house. When God sees you acting out the faith, He responds in a powerful way.

Let's focus on I John 5:5 for a moment. Apostle John asked a thought-provoking question, "Who is he that overcometh the world, but he that believeth that Jesus is the Son of God?" Who is the one that knocks down strong holds? Who are the ones that walk in homes and start envisioning where the furniture will go even though they cannot afford it? Who are the ones that pick out the car of their choice and demand a great rate when their credit is messed up? The answer, those who believe Jesus Christ is the Son of God!

Oftentimes we lose hope with God because we don't remember the promise. We often pray for things in general and don't know if God answered our prayers. Quit praying a general prayer to God. We never know if God answers our prayer when it's generic. Pray for things you can measure. King Jehoshaphat understood this concept. King Jehoshaphat and the Israelites were about to be attacked by two combined armies, the children of Moab and the children of Ammonites. He began to pray and remind God of the promise He made with Solomon. **II Chronicles 20:9** says, *"If, when evil cometh upon us, as the sword, judgment, or pestilence, or famine, we stand before this house, and in thy presence, (for thy name is in this house,) and cry unto thee in our affliction, then thou wilt hear and help."* King Jehoshaphat prays a clear and concise prayer to God. He reminded God of His promise to Solomon. God is faithful and just to keep all His promises. We must be obedient to line up with His promises. King Jehoshaphat was in the right line as well as lane to hear clearly from God. God responds to his prayer request in a powerful

> **Pray for things you can measure.**

way. **II Chronicles 20:15** says, *"And he said, Hearken ye, all Judah, and ye inhabitants of Jerusalem, and thou king Jehoshaphat, Thus saith the LORD unto you, Be not afraid nor dismayed by reason of this great multitude; for the battle is not yours, but God's."* The battle is not yours, but God's! Praise the Lord! God gave the assurance the battle was already won. God said this is not your fight. Listen closely, God does not want you fighting in the battle, He just needs you at the battlefield. The victory is already won. Don't bring a weapon; don't bring a sling shot, a spear, and don't bring a knife just open up your mouth with crazy praise. God wants you to see His glory. God wants you to know that when He defeats your enemy, you and the enemy will know it was God. **II Chronicles 20:17** says, *"Ye shall not need to fight in this battle: set yourselves, stand ye still, and see the salvation of the LORD with you, O Judah and Jerusalem: fear not, nor be dismayed; tomorrow go out against them: for the LORD will be with you."* The most amazing thing is that King Jehoshaphat believed the Lord. He bowed his head to the ground, and all Judah fell before the Lord in worship. Many people oftentimes praise God, but very few truly believe Him. King Jehoshaphat and the rest of Israel opened up their mouth and lifted up their voices and gave God a crazy, radical, and ridiculous praise. King Jehoshaphat received reve-

> **God does not want you fighting in the battle, he just needs you at the battlefield.**

lation from God. He and the Israelites let out praises unto God so loud it caused the devil to tremble.

I beseech you! I beg you! I am pleading with you to rise up from the ashes you've been laying. It is a brand new day! Let out the loudest and boldest praise you have ever released from your mouth. Now rise up from the mud you have been wallowing in and act upon your praise. You can't just praise God and don't move on your praise. We've been praising God for years and have not gotten the results we were expecting. You must put legs on your praise! King Jehoshaphat did just that. **II Chronicles 20:21** says, *"And when he had consulted with the people, he appointed singers unto the LORD, and that should praise the beauty of holiness, as they went out before the army, and to say, Praise the LORD; for his mercy endureth for ever."* King Jehoshaphat demonstrated his praise to God through his incredible faith walk. He was convinced God was going to show up in a mighty way. Notice, God did not assign the singers, King Jehoshaphat did. King Jehoshaphat wanted God to know he was not just a worshipper, but a doer of the Word! God absolutely enjoys singing and praise! God enjoys your faith even more! **Hebrews 11:6** says, *"But without faith it is impossible to please him: for he that cometh to God must believe that he is, and that he is a rewarder of them that diligently seek him."* Hebrews 11:6 is the scripture Voices of Faith Ministries was founded. We believe our voices are used to unleashing the power from within us (Holy

Spirit). Our faith must operate the power we summoned; therefore Voices of Faith Ministries was birth. It is in our faith where we benefit from the rewards of God. Remember while you are waiting on God, He is waiting on you! **II Chronicles 20:22** says, *"And when they began to sing and to praise, the LORD set ambushments against the children of Ammon, Moab, and mount Seir, which were come against Judah; and they were smitten."* This appointment of singers to lead the army into battle must have been in God's divine will, for as soon as they began to sing and praise God, He set ambushes against their enemy. Praise will confuse your enemy. Praise will cause your enemy to flee. As the Israelites were walking toward their enemy praising God, on the other side God was causing the enemy to fight one another. God just needs willing participants at the battle waiting and ready to pick up the spoil.

There is a pot of gold waiting for you at the end of your rainbow God designed for your life. God expects us to pursue it. Our obedience will propel us into our destiny. Walking in victory has its rewards! **II Chronicles 20:25** says, *"And when Jehoshaphat and his people came to take away the spoil of them, they found among them in abundance both riches with the dead bodies, and precious jewels, which they stripped off for themselves, more than they could carry away: and they were three days in gathering of the spoil, it was so much."* Because of the Israelites obedience, God rewarded their praise walking victory celebration. God did not promise your destiny was going to be a piece of cake, but He did promise if you are faithful and obedient, you will get to eat from the land. When God shows you a glimpse of your destiny, three things <u>must</u> be done to get there. **First**, we must worship God for the revelation and shout with a loud voice. **Second**, gather strength from prayer warriors and other faith walkers around you. **Third**, rise up early to move towards your destiny. The quicker you get started, the sooner you will arrive.

CHAPTER 8
FOR DISCUSSION

1. What is a prerequisite to walking in victory?

2. Why is it important for the devil to flatten your tires before the journey?

3. Describe the person who overcomes the world?

4. What does legs on your praise mean?

5. Why did King Jehoshaphat appoint singers to lead the army?

6. God just needs willing participants at the battle waiting and ready to pick up the _____.

7. What are three things that must be done after God shows you your destiny?

CONCLUSION

If you don't know by now, we must do whatever it takes to win. We must do whatever it takes to reach our destiny. We must fight for what's already ours. We must take back what the devil stole. Your destiny is depended upon your fight. If you refuse to fight, you have surrendered to the devil. He will forever use you as a punching bag beating you down whenever you try to get up. Satan knows he is in trouble if you are allowed to get on your feet. We are all playing on the same ball field with the same rules and regulations. The game of life has started, the clock is ticking away, and time is not your friend. Whether or not you choose to

> **Your destiny is depended upon your fight.**

enter the game, your name is still posted in the devil's locker room.

The difference between winners and losers; winners are pumped up for the challenge. They are risk takers and are extremely aggressive. They create fumbles and turnovers on their own. Winners take on life's problems head on. On the other hand, losers are looking for the perfect situation to enter the game. They run through life timid and unsure of themselves. Losers are waiting for their opponent to fumble and make a mistake. Losers are always complaining that life is unfair. The game of life is being played whether you choose to enter or not.

> **Winners take on life's problems head on.**

My name is on the roster. I have chosen to play the game that has been set before me. I have chosen to check in and fight for my destiny. I cannot depend on others. This is my assignment. I have been given a lane to operate. I understand the only way to complete my mission is to strap on the uniform and fight for it. I know there will be punches thrown my way, but I plan on throwing more than the enemy. I now have on the proper equipment. I am covered in the blood of Jesus Christ. My relationship with God is intact. I know that no weapon formed against me shall prosper. I want my destiny! I am desperate to reach my destiny! Don't you want yours? I need it and cannot think of anything else until I achieve it.

There is a purpose for your life. Find out yours!

God wants to fulfill your purpose and crown you with heaven's greatest reward. When I get to heaven, I am looking to pick up my life time achievement award! It will read, "Well done my good and faithful servant — God." Paul said it best in **II Timothy 4:7-8**, *"I have fought a good fight, I have finished my course, I have kept the faith. Henceforth there is laid up for me a crown of righteousness, which the Lord, the righteous judge, shall give me at that day: and not to me only, but unto all them also that love his appearing."* Remember, your race has already been won, your ship has already come in, and your flight has already landed. Your job is to FIGHT FOR YOUR DESTINY! "Be strong and of a good courage."

CONCLUSION
FOR DISCUSSION

1. What will happen if you refuse to fight the devil?

2. What is the difference between winners and losers?

3. What will be on your life time achievement award in heaven?

4. No _____ formed against me shall prosper.

5. Is time your best friend? Why?

6. The game of life has started, have you checked in yet?

7. Are you fighting your best fight and running your course?

BIBLIOGRAPHY

Barnett, Tommy
Hidden Power
Lake Mary, Florida: Charisma House Publishers, 2002.

Cobbins, Tony D.
Spiritual Storm Chasers
Niles, Illinois: Mall Publishing, Co., 2003.

Dollar, Creflo A.
Uprooting The Spirit of Fear
Tulsa, Oklahoma: Harrison House, Inc. Publishers, 1994.

Hagin, Kenneth E.
Understanding The Anointing
Tulsa, Oklahoma: Faith Library Publications, 1996.

Hansel, Tim
Eating Problems For Breakfast
Dallas, Texas: Word Publishing, 1988.

Marriott, J.W.
The Spirit To Serve
New York, New York: HarperCollins Publishers, 1997.

Maxwell, John C.
Failing Forward
Nashville, Tennessee: Thomas Nelson Publishers, 2000.

Maxwell, John C.
Running With The Giants
Orange, California: An AOL Time Warner Company, Warner Books, 2002.

Price, Fred
How Faith Works
Tulsa, Oklahoma: Harrison House, Inc. Publishers, 1976.

Richards, Larry
When Life Is Unfair
Dallas, Texas: Word Publishing, 1989

Tenney, Tommy
The God Chasers
Shippensburg, Pennsylvania: Destiny Image Publishers, Inc. 1998.

Tozer, A.W.
The Knowledge of the Holy
New York, New York: HarperCollins Publishers, 1992.